SHADE GARDENS

COMPLETE GARDENER'S LIBRARY™

SHADE

GARDENS

Mimi Luebbermann

NATIONAL HOME
GARDENING CLUB

National Home
Gardening Club
Minnetonka, Minnesota

Shade Gardens

Tom Carpenter
Director of Book Development

Julie Cisler
Book Design & Production

Michele Teigen
Senior Book Development Coordinator

Gina Germ
Photo Editor

Shari Gross
Production Coordinator

Laura Belpedio
Book Development Assistant

Nancy Wirsig McClure, Hand to Mouse Arts
Illustration

5 6 7 8 / 05 04 03 02
ISBN 1-58159-016-4

National Home Gardening Club
12301 Whitewater Drive
Minnetonka, Minnesota 55343
www.gardeningclub.com

Photo Credits

   Jim Block pp. cover, i, 6, 7, 20, 21(3), 22, 33, 38-39, 41, 42, 47(2), 48, 49(3), 52, 54, 59, 63, 64, 65, 68-69, 74, 75 both, 81, 82, 94, 103, 104, 105, 112, 113(4), 115(2), 116, 117(3), 123, 125 all, 126(2), 128, 131(2), 133, 136 all, 139, 141(2), 142, 146, 147, 148, 149, 160; **Walter Chandoha** pp. ii, 4(2), 5, 6, 14, 15(2), 16, 18(2), 19, 20, 21, 23 all, 24, 25, 29, 30 both, 31, 33(2), 35, 36 both, 37, 40, 43, 45(2), 48, 49, 50 both, 51 all, 53 both, 54, 55, 56, 57 both, 58 both, 59, 60, 61, 62, 67, 79, 83, 84, 87, 90, 94, 103, 108, 110, 111, 113, 114, 115, 118, 122, 127, 131, 137, 148, 149(3), 150 both, 151 both, 152 all, 153, 154, 155, 156, 158 both, 159, 161(2), 162 both, 163; **Derek Fell** pp. vi, 73, 76 both, 77 all, 78, 84, 87, 89, 91 both, 93, 95(2), 96 all, 97 all, 101(2), 102 both, 103, 107 both, 108, 112, 114, 115, 118, 119(2), 120 both, 121 both, 123, 126, 130, 132, 133, 137(3), 138, 139(2), 141, 142; **William D. Adams** pp. 2-3, 8, 11, 19, 25, 45, 54, 59, 66, 72, 83, 85, 86 both, 88 both, 89(2), 92, 95, 104, 114, 116, 119(2), 123, 124, 127, 141(2), 143, 153, 159, 161; **Mark Turner** pp. 4, 6, 29, 44, 47, 81, 92, 98, 99, 101, 132, 137, 138, 139, 140, 147; **Hugh Palmer** pp. 5, 6(2), 8, 10, 11, 12-13, 15, 16, 18, 26-27, 31, 32, 37, 41, 46, 67, 80, 105, 106, 108, 112, 130, 138; **Jerry Pavia** pp. 7, 17, 34-35, 42, 43, 49, 61, 63, 71, 81, 94, 109, 111, 129; ©**Positive Images:** Lee Anne White p. 9, Jerry Howard pp. 11, 129, 147, Karen Bussolini p. 14, Pam Spaulding pp. 17, 106, 129, Patricia J. Bruno p. 19, Jim Kahnweiler p. 48, Margaret Hensel pp. 60, 79, 134, Ben Philips p. 73, Albert Squillace p. 128; **Michael Landis** pp. 10, 11, 15, 18, 19, 31, 66, 67, 72(2), 74, 99, 100, 132, 133, 134, 135, 140, 143, 144-145, 146, 154, 157; **Saxon Holt** pp. 28, 63, 74, 110; **Joseph P. Strauch, Jr.** pp. 41, 65, 71, 78, 79, 89, 92, 93, 100, 104, 109(2), 117, 129, 130, 140; **Horticultural Photography, Mountain View, CA** pp. 70 both, 143; **Bill Johnson** pp. 80, 118, 127, 128; **Amy Sumner** p. 163; **Matthew Plut** p. 1.

CONTENTS

ABOUT THE AUTHOR

At 11 I fell in love with shade gardens. An older sister was getting married and as the wedding was in New York, my family drove up from our home in tropical Florida. I, too excited to sleep the morning after our late night arrival, crept out to explore the garden of a borrowed house. Everything in the garden smelled morning fresh and sweet, with the dew lingering on the leaves. I discovered a shady brick path that beckoned me around to the back of the house and down through the garden. Large trees towered overhead, and along the path's edges were flowering bushes—it was very different than Florida.

The sunlight freckled my path, and I came to its end in the midst of a large peony garden. The pink and white blooms seem in my memory to bend toward me at eye level, with the elegant fineness of the thin petals surrounding a burst of egg-yellow stamens, and of course, their sweet peony fragrance seemed to envelop me in waves. I lingered to inhale their perfume, and then skipped back up my beautiful path.

To this day, gardens with a shady path always seem irresistible, full of promise of a surprise at the end. Shade gardens promise a cooling invitation to rest from sizzling heat, protection from the full glare of the sun, a haven of rest and meditation. Their cool, dimly-lit areas offer refreshment and allure, the promise of stepping into another world.

One of the most impressive shade gardens I ever visited belonged to an elderly friend who had gardened all her life. Her tiny garden in the warm summer area of the San Francisco region was shaded by encircling native trees—tall madrones, bay trees and oaks. She used

cymbidiums in pots for late winter accents, packed her planting spaces with daffodils and azaleas and placed fragrant rhododendrons along paths for spring bloom. She filled holes with ferns, Christmas roses and drifts of fleabane. In summer, large planters with ivy and red and white geraniums along the edge of the concrete patio bloomed amiably in the mixed shade. It was an easy, low-maintenance garden with the punch of bloom throughout the year.

As a gardener in Northern California, I struggled to garden successfully for years with a narrow urban lot. The location parceled out sunlight variously throughout the seasons, producing scores of microclimates from month to month. Some areas received direct sun early in the morning or late afternoon in the summertime only. Others blistered with sun from sunup to sundown. The entry garden's morning light was blocked by a neighbor's towering incense cedar but, in the afternoon, the westering sunlight was pitiless.

It took me years of experimenting to find plants delighted

with their surroundings and satisfied with the type of light they received regardless of the season. One of my most successful plantings was underneath the veil of a large tree, which I planted with camellias. Under those grew old-fashioned campanulas and running iris given to me by a septuagenarian gardener. Shade-happy succulents turned out to be garden heroes, adapting to different sun quantities from season to season, drought tolerant and happy to spread themselves throughout the border over the years.

Now, when fellow gardeners groan to me as they describe their garden as shady-dark, I surprise them with my enthusiastic response: How lucky you are, and what a great opportunity to grow some of the best plants! Vegetable gardeners bemoaning lack of sunlight can take heart, for many edible plants grow in light shade or part shade, from a variety of lettuces to fruit trees. I grew plums, apples and pears in my little city garden in a location where they got some direct morning sun, but were in part shade all afternoon long.

So take heart. Shade gardens are a treasure and you can pack them full of glorious plants. Besides, in the heat of a summer's day, who wants to be out there in the full blast of the sunshine weeding and digging? Who doesn't long for a fine rough tree trunk back support underneath a shading tree to sip a glass of ice-cold water and appreciate the garden of one's efforts.

Mimi Luebbermann

◀ CHAPTER 1 ▶
AN INTRODUCTION TO SHADE

The glories of shade are quickly established. Call to mind a blistering hot summer day, the sweat beginning to trickle off your forehead, and then imagine a tall glass of lemonade with clinking ice cubes and a softly pillowed lounge chair. Where would you place the chair—out in the harsh dazzle of full sunlight? Oh no, we would immediately drag that chair into the cool repose of a shady spot.

Shade beckons to us. Shade clothes us in a silky coolness that provides a sense of ease while invoking a kind of mysterious air. In contrast, a sunny garden holds no hidden secrets. Plus, the full blast of the sun flattens out flower colors, which in the shade take on a neon brightness. White in sunshine seems harshly flat; but in a shaded garden bed, white flowers shimmer like the beam of a flashlight at night.

A WORLD OF SHADY PLACES

The dark green woodland garden serves as a backdrop for the red and pink flowers of rhododenrons. The light pink color in the foreground leads the eye back to the dark red in the background, creating the illusion of great distance—a handy trick to make small gardens seem larger.

Every home garden has shady areas to transform into glorious shade gardens. It makes sense of course, that many plants all over the world bask in the shade—growing lush, vibrant foliage and flowers. Just thinking of woodland groves, dense wooded canyons and dappled light on the forest floor or along shaded brooks calls to mind all the different ecological regions of the world where sun peeps in through trees. Over the vast rush of geologic time, thousands of plants have adapted to low-light environments. Consequently, shade gardens, imitating the macrocosm under nature's tree canopies (whether in tropical jungles or suburban backyards) host an incredible variety of plants.

In shaded areas, gardeners have an opportunity to grow gorgeous plants for bloom or foliage and,

depending upon the exposure, even for edible plantings. There are endless possibilities for a shady spot to become a special destination in your garden complete with a seating area, gazebo or garden pavilion that provides shade. For those with limited garden space, a potted garden on a shady veranda can flaunt year-round blooms. Fire escapes or rooftops can also become verdant with growing plants.

Learning How to Measure Shade

Plants have different light—as opposed to sunlight—requirements. Light, as you would measure it with a camera's light meter, is quite different from direct sunlight shining on a plant, or even dappled sun playing over the surface of a plant's leaves. Some plants naturally prefer lower light levels; if they are exposed to high levels of light, their leaves burn as sensitively as winter-whitened skin on the first day at the beach. Learning to judge the qualities of shade

Create relaxing places where you can sit and enjoy your garden. Plant fragrant flowers next to the spot, or change it with containers of annuals.

The comfort of shade encourages easy conversation.

North

| 1 Dappled Shade | 2 Open Shade | 3 Medium Shade | 4 Deep Shade |

and the different amounts of light will help you locate just the right spot in your garden to encourage the healthy growth of a particular plant. For the gardener's convenience, shade is designated with the numbers 1 to 4 to indicate the density of the shade. The number 1 indicates the lightest amount of shade and the number 4 the darkest.

Light or Dappled Shade, Shade 1 is bright enough that most plants, including those with directions to grow in full sun, will tolerate light shade. The sunlight moves across the space, dappling the ground underneath, but never remaining as full sunlight for any length of time.

Open Shade, Shade 2 can be found in a narrow side yard with a northern exposure. Although the light is bright, there is rarely any direct sun. Underneath a patio covered with fiberglass or a shade cloth provides the same kind of light. Although many plants tolerate this shade level, it can be too diminished for plants that like full sun.

Medium Shade, Shade 3 begins to sort out plants that only tolerate shade and shifts to plants that prefer shade. This type of shade is found under small trees that are themselves under a canopy tree, under decks and stairwells, and in a north-facing side garden that has trees blocking any sunlight.

Deep Shade, Shade 4 limits the plant selection to those hardy plants such as ivy or moss which need very limited light to survive. Many of the plants that live in deep shade grow slowly and rarely bloom. Deep shade can be found in narrow garden areas where light is blocked by trees, fences and buildings.

Shade plants in containers dress up walkways, stairways and patios. Change annuals from season to season or mix annuals and perennials. For best results, keep containers consistently watered.

Seating places in the shade invite a restful interlude.

Even a tiny water garden attracts birds and dragonflies—creating life and movement in your garden, terrace or balcony garden.

Watch the patterns of shade different trees throw all through the day, and through the different seasons. Knowing your shade patterns will help you plan your planting scheme.

A pathway meanders past grasses, gravel and rocks in a Japanese-style garden.

Matching Plants to Your Shady Areas

The quality and quantity of shade changes throughout the year because of the tilting of the earth's axis and the subsequent changing position of the sun. The shade gardener must observe pools of garden shade to measure how they change from season to season as the sun drops lower in the southern sky during winter and then migrates in a northern axis during the long days of summer. A plant set in a shady spot in early April may be burning up in full sun by August because of this shift in sunlight. The angle of the sun also changes in relationship to the distance a garden stands from the equator. Consequently gardens in Texas experience different sun angles

versus those in Minnesota. Careful observation to track the sun's path and the shade cast in your garden allows you to match your plants' shade needs to the shade available in your garden.

Making the Most of Shade

There are special gardening techniques to help you increase success in your shaded garden areas. Once you understand the basics of shade, you may find you can alter the amount of light that comes into your shady garden bed.

Lawns with changing shade patterns still receive enough light to grow successfully.

New hardier types of camellias are available, now making them suited to cold-weather gardens. Don't miss out on tender old-fashioned varieties—just grow them in containers and move them into a protected area over the winter.

Use your shade garden like another room in the house—an added space for relaxing pursuits or as an antidote to the workday.

Choose plants for your garden to provide interest at different seasons of the year. Here fall leaves show off as much color as spring bloom.

Judicious pruning, increasing light by using walls and fences and matching up the light in different seasons to garden plants stretches your choices of plants to grow in the shade. For instance, a spring bulb garden underneath a grove of maple trees gives you a glorious spring display that fades away as the trees leaf out later in spring. The trees then filter out the sunlight that produced the spring display. All of these techniques are explained later in the book and will help to introduce you to a wider variety of plants.

Latitude and Shade

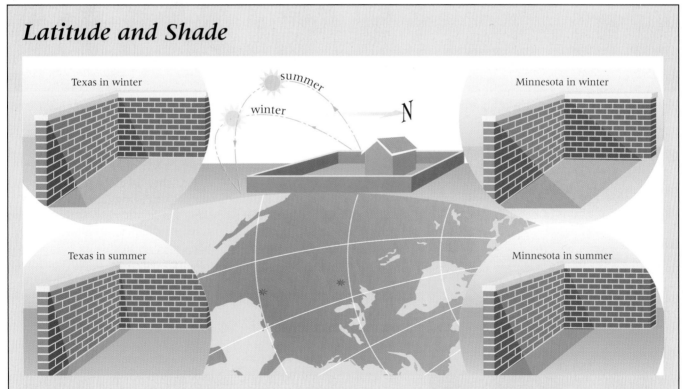

Texas in winter

summer

winter

N

Minnesota in winter

Texas in summer

Minnesota in summer

Shade isn't as simple as it might seem. Learn to watch the amount and quality of shade a spot receives through the day—as well as through the seasons—before selecting your plants. The sun's angle changes drastically—and many shade-loving plants don't stand for severe changes. Keep in mind that latitude, the angle of the sun in various seasons and changes in deciduous trees can all cause shade to differ. In fact, areas beneath some trees may have full sun until the trees completely leaf out in spring.

MAKING SHADE

Azaleas parading along the edge of an arbor benefit from the shade it throws, and soften the effect of the very geometrical structure.

A shady bench is the perfect destination for a cup of morning coffee or afternoon tea.

For those whose gardens don't offer enough shade, you can build structures to protect sun-tender plants, either as a temporary solution or a permanent addition to your landscape. Lath houses protect the tender foliage of begonias and fuchsias from searing summer sun. Simple bamboo structures built just for one summer season and covered with annual flowering vines can make a hidden retreat to shield a lounge chair or picnic table. Shade cloth over a simple plastic pipe structure makes a summer greenhouse or outdoor lounge area.

Planting trees to take over the job of providing shade necessitates a realistic assessment of the amount of space available to an adult tree. Something that seems a mere twig now in only a few short years can become a giant, threatening a house foundation, a roof or blotting out sun for myriad favorite shrubs and perennial plantings. With vines, an equally important consideration is providing structure to support the adult vine. A spindly vine can, as a bulky adult, pull over light structures or simply crush them with the burden of spring's rampant growth of limbs and leaves.

No matter where the shade comes from, what makes a garden really work is more than just well-cared-for plants. Instead it's fitting them into a master plan that pieces together all the elements of garden design—your needs, site and personal style. Taking the time to map out your garden and plan for changes and updating produces a garden with a sense of unity and design that plays off colors and textures, and makes a place of beauty.

The "Collection of Shade Gardens" (pages 38-67) pictured in this book are meant to be an inspiration for the gardener, filled with ideas to

A pathway leading straight to the doorway of the gazebo invites you to stroll in.

Trees and Shade

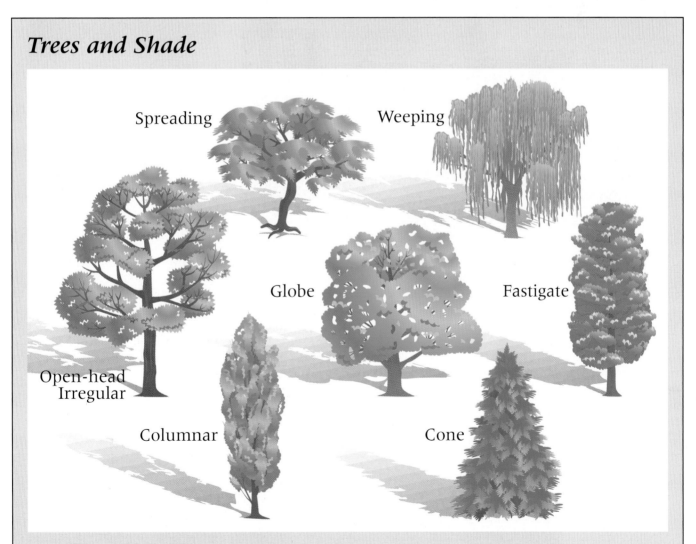

Spreading

Weeping

Globe

Fastigate

Open-head
Irregular

Columnar

Cone

Trees throw different types of shadows. Tall columnar trees provide a striking vertical accent in the garden but send out only a thin sliver of shade. A round-headed Japanese maple creates an umbrella of shade, although the small leaves let light filter through. A large-leaved maple makes an extensive shadow and the large, thick leaves make it very dense. Look carefully at your choices before you make your decision.

An arbor, freestanding or connected to a fence, creates vertical lines in the garden. An arbor is the perfect excuse to grow roses or vines.

A garden gazebo sits grandly at the end of a path. Every garden should have a destination spot—whether a simple rustic bench or an elegant shade structure.

transplant into your own garden. Work up plant lists most appropriate for your own area. Don't forget to make use of your local nursery experts or your county extension agent. Catalogs are great resources for new and unusual plants not available from local nurseries. Try raising plants from seed to bring unusual specimens into your garden.

Our encyclopedia section of "Plants for the Shade Garden" (pages 68-143) suggests widely available plants to tuck into your garden. Choose plants for your garden using the information later in the book on soil preparation and planting, the qualities of shade and light, as well as the light requirements of shade-loving or shade-tolerant plants. Three of the most important points to consider are the amount of light the plant requires for healthy growth, the weather it needs and the moisture it must have to grow in your garden area.

COLORS IN THE SHADE

Colors in shade are intensified. Light colors such as bright green, chartreuse, light pink and white seem to shimmer, appearing closer than they really are. In comparison, dark green recedes, making the plant seem farther back in the shade. Separating masses of conflicting colors with a block of white makes the colors seem more harmonious. Placing light colors behind dark colors at the back of the border makes the border look wider. White in Shade 3 areas creates the illusion of a light source in a dark area.

Lattice panels provide shade as well as structure for growing plants. Mandevilla 'Alice du Pont' grown in containers stays small but is covered in pink blooms all summer long.

Bring shade to the garden wherever you want it.

You may be able to locate what is not available from your local nursery or garden store in the specialty mail-order catalogs given in the sources section.

Lastly, a plea for breaking the rules. Once you have read about design and about color and placement, try out the concepts exactly—just as you would try out a recipe for the first time. Then break some rules. Try large plants in front of small ones in the border, play with growing roses in fruit trees, experiment with a garden bed of multicolored lettuces or pair flowering kale and pansies. Why not?

Remember, gardening is meant to be fun and provide pleasure; getting stuck planting the same old things year after year becomes drudgery.

The glory of shade gardens awaits you, filled with the adventure of new plants in new colors all ready to be set into the shady areas of your garden. The alluring world off the stage of bright sunshine awaits you with a whole host of shade-loving plants to star in every shady corner of your garden.

Tall canopy trees bring shade to house and garden. Deciduous trees allow sunlight to warm the house in winter; when leafed out in summer, they provide cooling shade.

There should always be some time to put off garden chores. Otherwise, gardens become all work with no pleasure.

◆ CHAPTER 2 ◆
BRINGING SHADE TO THE GARDEN

All gardens and all gardening conditions are not the same. In some gardens the sun is brilliant and warm in the morning, but by afternoon cool winds make the garden uncomfortable. In others, throbbing heat makes garden work impossible after midmorning unless it is in the shade. Although some gardeners are forced to cope with an abundance of shade in their gardens, others find that they have too much sizzling sun, mercilessly beating down on them and their plants.

A gardener must come up with a plan, a series of strategies to manage shade to the garden's best advantage. If you have too much shade, modify your shade through pruning or even tree removal. If you have too much sun, then you will want to develop shade. In the short term you can introduce shade-producing structures; in the long term, plant shrubs and trees that will bring the grace of shade to the garden as well as blossoms, fragrance and even fruit if you so wish.

STRUCTURES TO CREATE SHADE

Although trees bring the loveliest shade into the garden, they are not always practical. If you are planting a canopy tree to create shade, you will wait for at least five years to receive any benefit and longer still until it reaches arching, shade-producing maturity. In small gardens a large tree is unthinkable, considering it may crane over rooftops or impinge upon scanty sun areas. Structures (such as these described here) bring more immediate results without the drawbacks.

The Advantages of Structures

Structures bring in patches of shade through the day and enhance the garden in a variety of other ways. Perhaps a gardener is a fancier of clematis or other vines, or longs for a fragrant haven filled with the scent of honeysuckle. Pergolas or arbors can serve as great additional growing spaces draped with vines that offer bloom, fragrance and even fruit while supplying a pool of dappled shade underneath. Additionally, in mild winter climates where a gardener can risk growing half-hardy plants, the chilling frosts have less effect underneath an arbor.

On a hot summer day, a patio's shaded overhead brings relief from soaring temperatures; when situated by west-facing windows, a patio can cut off the burning glare of the afternoon sun to leave the house cooler through the day. A wooden lath house shelters tender plants like begonias that would otherwise burn up in direct sunlight. In the heat of the day, a trip into the sweet cool of the lath house with a glass of iced tea introduces civility into a sweltering day.

Designing Structures Suited to Your Site

Structures, as architectural elements in the garden, add great beauty and focal points of interest. So it is important to

Roses clothe an arbor for bloom and shade. Perpetual blooming types repeat bloom after their spring outburst. Look for disease-resistant varieties for easy maintenance.

'New Dawn' roses climb 15 feet high and will spread 10 feet wide to ramble over structures. Particularly suited to hot steamy summers, the climber blooms all summer long with small, lightly fragrant pink blossoms that fade to white as they open.

A rustic arbor brings a bit of whimsy to the garden. Early colonial gardens usually included a rustic arbor using timbers on hand. Make sure the arbor is well constructed for long-lasting results.

A gazebo can be designed in different styles to set the tone for the garden or to match a garden design. This Japanese-style gazebo, set in the woods, becomes a destination for a stroll through the garden.

design them well before introducing them. If built of wood, the structures must be sturdy and strong. A delicate arbor built with lightweight wood and festooned with wisteria

Two cheerful, red-striped umbrellas bring shade where it is needed regardless of the sun's location. Umbrellas, available in many different colors and shapes, bring color to a deck or patio.

looks lovely when the vines are young. As the vines age, they swell and grow heavy with weight. Many a gardener has come out after a heavy summer rain to find an arbor collapsed with the weight of the old vine sodden with rain and pushed by wind.

Consider what weatherproofing techniques are appropriate, for if an arbor is to be covered with plants it may not be practical to use paint as a protectant, as it must be renewed regularly through the years. To strip off plants to repaint it can be laborious and injurious for the plants. Protect the footings against rot and subsequent collapse through use of cement or nontoxic wood preservatives. Keeping soil and moisture away from the wood helps protect against rot and infestation by termites and other wood-eating insects.

Many companies now produce kits for different garden structures. There are pergolas,

overhead archways, gazebos and lath houses that can be ordered through the mail and arrive ready to assemble in a weekend. See "Sources," page 164, for companies providing such a service. Remember though, that some of the most charming structures are simple and rustic, often homemade from trimmed branches and recycled wood. A garden structure does not necessarily need to be elaborate or expensive to provide shade and beauty.

For the greatest gardening and entertaining flexibility, consider covering only part of a patio.

TYPES OF SHADE STRUCTURES

If you have ever traveled in Central America, the American South or even old Western towns, you will find the sidewalks are covered to protect walkers from the searing heat of the midday sun. Long ago in China, a tile-covered walkway known as a *lang* crossed gardens sometimes in straight lines or sometimes zig-zagging through open spaces. Like covered sidewalks, langs connected buildings, keeping the walkers in cool shade or protected from monsoon rains.

Gardeners have long erected simple structures to create shady retreats in their gardens during the hot summer days. If you like to linger near the kitchen in the morning or as dusk creeps in, then perhaps a shaded seating area off the kitchen would be a good location for a shade structure. A shady spot on a garden path makes a destination in the garden, whether it is a bench under a canopy of climbing red roses drooping over a simple wire and wood framework, or an umbrella shielding chairs and surrounded by pots bursting with tuberous begonias. Larger shade structures can become the favorite spot to linger over Saturday morning coffee or to host a Sunday night supper served off the barbecue.

Arbors or Pergolas

Arbors and pergolas are simple structures that provide overhead shade to a walkway. They must be built to withstand the weight of plants, and to stand up to stormy winds. They can project off a house or be self-standing. Some of the most delightful arbors are made with rustic tree limbs. Although they

Matching garden structures to the plants they will support is essential. The weight of an old wisteria can pull down a flimsy arbor.

look simple, they must be carefully constructed because if poorly made, they soon collapse. Other inexpensive and easily manufactured arbors are made from plastic or metal pipe painted green or black, and then covered with a combination of vines.

No matter what kind of arbor you choose, remember to design it in proportion to the garden space and consistent with the garden design. An arbor in a Japanese-style garden would take clues on its details from garden buildings or pavilions built in the Japanese style. A rustic, cottage garden needs an informal arbor, perhaps using tree branches or fence-post rounds instead of the more formal square shapes of milled lumber. In a small garden, a lacy

A loosely woven lattice or an open pergola allows fruit or blooms to dangle through attractively.

Oakleaf hydrangeas love the shade of an arbor, and enclose it with bloom and interesting leaf texture.

ironwork arbor would be more appropriate than a heavy, large arbor which would outweigh the size of the garden and loom over it uncomfortably.

Use care when choosing plants to cover the arbor. Remember that vines can become so rampant that they strangle the arbor, obscuring its design and leaving such dense shade underneath that few plants will grow. If an arbor is shading house windows from the sun's summer glare, use a deciduous vine, which lets sun in during the cold winter months.

Also, don't forget trees and shrubs with supple, flexible limbs such as sasanqua camellias or *Rhododendron* x *fragrantissimum* that can be trained up and over an arbor or pergola. These plants may present a better choice than a rampant vine. You can even train fruit trees to cover a pergola for blossom, shade, fruit and

fall color. Although using a single type of plant to cover an arbor presents a unified look, you may prefer to choose a variety of plants such as clematis and climbing roses for continued interest through the whole growing season.

For maintenance, the arbor plants—particularly perennial vines—need to be trained and pruned annually. Perennial vines can become woody, losing their leaves and only presenting tangled growth. Prune the vines annually to keep the arbor looking its best. Check the correct time of year to prune a specific plant, for pruning at the wrong time may shear off emerging blossoms.

A Shaded Patio

There is nothing more delightful than spending time on a shaded patio, whether eating a meal, relaxing in a lounge chair or even taking a nap on a Sunday afternoon. Direct sunlight on a stifling day sends anyone back into the house, which may be even warmer. Designing a patio with access into a house expands the living area, adding another room to your home. Many gardeners in hot summer areas declare they spend more time on their patios than inside the house. Design your covered

An open arbor overhung with a roof of vines becomes a gazebo perfect for growing tender shade plants such as begonias and impatiens. A deciduous vine may leave plants too exposed to sun when it has dropped its leaves. Keep an eye on plants to judge the effect of the light on them.

patio with the following points in mind—how you anticipate using the space, your budget, the amount of maintenance you want and whether it should be waterproof. Covering a patio makes it more usable in all kinds of weather.

Natural and Synthetic Cloth Covers

The most natural cover for a patio is an arbor hung with vines. The choice of vines is important because fruiting vines may attract wasps and flies unless the fruit is harvested promptly. Deciduous vines with dropping leaves mean regular sweeping to keep the patio livable. Evergreen vines make good choices as long as you prune to allow light to filter into the patio.

One of the simplest fabric patio covers is a canvas cover either in white or in a variety of stripes or solid colors. Colors will fade and canvas, if kept out long past the summer, may be subject to mildew, even though many commercially produced cloths have anti-mildew protection

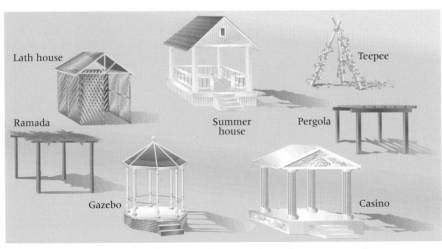

There are a lot of garden structures available to choose from. Be sure the structures match the feel of your garden and, more importantly, your personal taste.

A striped canvas canopy makes a stylish rooftop to an outdoor living space. A classic solution to overly hot patios, the cotton allows good air circulation while blocking the sun's rays.

added for longer wear. But canvas protects against gentle summer rain showers so you can keep patio cushions in place. There are also new acrylic canvases that are long-lasting and rot-resistant.

Make sure the cloth is hung and fastened to stand up to summer storms and winds. In some cases you may need to design a covering with panels of canvas instead of one solid piece, both to allow better air circulation and, in windy locations, to prevent tearing. A badly designed covering can trap warm air, making the patio hotter than without the cover. Also available are canvas shades that you can pull out and adjust depending upon the angle of the sun.

Another choice is shade cloth—originally designed as a light penetrating cloth for green-

houses. This cloth, still used in commercial greenhouses, lets different amounts of light filter in, depending upon the cloth's weave. It can be ordered in different sizes with grommets and bound edges for convenient and long-lasting wear. Shade cloth does shrink approximately one to three percent, so when you measure to order it, add enough to allow the cloth to tighten and not tear after its first wetting in a rain storm. Keep in mind—shade cloth can also increase the temperature on the patio, as it was designed to trap heat in greenhouses.

A Wooden Slat Covering

Consider a wooden lath covering, which provides shade *and* allows air to circulate. Lath allows branches to creep through, from cascading roses to clusters of grapes. Redwood laths have a long life, and will last even longer if you apply a wood preservative before construction. Although they can be painted white to reflect more light into the space, remember that painted wood surfaces must be repainted. This can be labor intensive and expensive. Fiberglass lath panels are

now available too. They are light, long-lasting and never have to be painted. The panels can be hung in such a way that they can be unfastened and removed over the winter. Many lumber stores carry these kinds of panels.

Fiberglass Panels

Solid fiberglass panels and plastic panels come in rippled or flat sheets; typical installations make them more permanent than other types of patio coverings. Consider the following when purchasing fiberglass panels: There are some types of fiberglass that block ultraviolet rays,

Although this narrow, high-walled patio would be shaded in the morning and evening, at high noon an umbrella brings shady relief to what would otherwise be an unbearably hot and bright situation.

In this tropical courtyard, an umbrella brings shade to the seating area.

Lath houses don't have any one classical shape. This special lath house stands out as an unusual building with its graceful shape. The small leaves of the vine do not obscure its structure.

This gazebo highlights an entry to the pool. Designed to be in proportion to its backdrop, it is built on quite massive proportions to match the two-story house in the background. When designing your garden, always create the proportions of the structure in relationship to its surroundings.

making the material unsuitable for growing any plants underneath. Others stop direct sunlight but allow the ultraviolet rays to travel through. The light that comes through fiberglass panels is quite pleasant, but affected by the color of the panel. Try propping up panels at the lumberyard and let the light through the different colors, giving yourself a chance to judge the quality of light thrown off.

A pathway leads to a Victorian-style gazebo.

Bamboo Shades

A temporary covering, such as bamboo or woven reeds, makes a casual topping to a small patio. But make sure not to purchase types held together with cotton string, for it quickly frays and causes the shade to fall apart; instead look for bamboo shades made with metal. These shades, folded up and put away over fall and winter, can be reused for a number of years.

Gazebos

The Oxford Companion to Gardens suggests that the word "gazebo" comes from "facetious Latin" meaning to gaze. It says the gazebo should be situated on a rise to overlook the garden, or be raised up for a better view. A small detached room for gazing is a lovely thing in a garden, making a place to sit and contemplate, or simply to enjoy the garden. The Victorians crafted gazebos with intricate woodwork for the express purpose of taking tea. Comfortable rocking chairs and tea tables furnished these gazing rooms, which might be more properly called "grazing" rooms. As an ornament to the garden, a gazebo can be simple or complex, large or small. Interwoven with vines or shaded by trees, the gazebo is a treasure in anyone's garden.

Lath House

A lath house uses strips of wood pieces—lath is usually $1/2$ inch by 2 inches by any number of lengths—to create a room with just the amount of dappled shade beloved

A white-painted ornate gazebo stands out from the green forest backdrop to make an architectural statement in the garden.

by tuberous begonias, fuchsias, ferns, orchids and house plants that need summering outside. A lath house is a cool oasis, and the flowers and fresh green of ferns make it a haven during the summer months. If your climate is hot and dry, you may want to locate the lath house underneath the shade of a tall tree. If you are growing plants in the lath house, consider installing an automatic misting system to protect them from dry heat. Easily installed, small misters send out a spray that refreshes humidity-loving plants.

Panels of unpainted or prepainted and nailed lath are available from lumberyards to make construction easier. Lath houses can be simple or elegant depending upon your design and your needs. Design your house as a utilitarian plant house, maintaining shade plants until they are ready for display; or make the house a destination on a garden stroll, complete with plants wondrously in bloom and a table for taking a meal.

This lath house creates an opportunity for shade both inside and along the edges.

VINES AS SHADE STRUCTURES

Vines clambering over structures bring quick shade to the garden. Match the mature size of the plant to the space. If the vine outgrows the space, you'll have to prune the vine back to size.

Vines can quickly provide shade for the garden. These plants dress up shade structures with their long, flexible arms, and they twine or climb up and over structures to soften their angles, covering them in colorful blooms or bright fall leaves. Vines can be deciduous or evergreen, annuals or perennials. Even some shrubs with open, lanky growth are used as "vines" as long as the gardener is willing to guide and tie the long branches along an arbor or lath house. Vines bloom with hundreds of small flowers such as passionflower, wisteria or honeysuckle ... or great dinner-plate-sized ones like some varieties of clematis. Grapes, kiwi or passionflower vines serve up edible fruit, and types such as

Virginia creeper provide brilliant crimson fall color. And consider the fragrance of *Clematis armandii*, with waves of vanilla-scented perfume. Jasmine planted to grow around a bedroom window scents your night's slumbers.

Bear in mind—not all vines climb the same way. Some vines such as ivy have little attaching rootlets that latch on to any flat structure to hold the weight of the vine. Although this means the gardener doesn't have to tie up the vine, it means that should it ever become necessary to remove the vine, an unsightly trail of these sticky

feet will be left on the wall. In the case of painting a house, you will first have to sand extensively to remove these sticky feet; this could be costly.

Other vines produce twining tendrils that reach out and grab support, as long as there is something for them to twine around such as a post, wire or string. Grapevines grow with such tendrils, so providing netting or wire is essential to support these vines.

Other plants, such as beans, grow with the whole vine curling around the support. Care must be taken to notice the direction of the curl. If you try to force a plant in the opposite way, you can break off the head of the plant.

Note that vines grow to different lengths. Some of the honeysuckles will spread out along a whole property fence-line, others grow only to 10 feet. Choose the plant for the space you have, and make sure your support can hold its weight as it grows older and becomes heavier.

Sturdy poles anchor this rustic arbor to firm up a somewhat flimsy structure. It is hard for gardeners to imagine that the little, new grape plants will mature to 15- to 20-feet-long vines, possibly causing the arbor to collapse under their weight.

PLANTING TREES AND TALL SHRUBS

Flowering trees add a special dimension to any garden.

habits. Some trees drop leaves all year long or unwanted seedpods after bloom. Others send out surface roots that invade all the best flower borders, competing for growing space. Trees may promote allergies with a heavy pollen count in the spring.

There are two kinds of trees to consider for the shade garden. There are small trees suitable for a small urban garden or underneath a canopy of taller trees. These trees must tolerate shade, must be able to live next to a taller neighboring tree or accept limited light due to buildings that block out the sun. Then there are the tall canopy trees, trees that stretch up and overshadow a garden.

Many fruit trees grow well with just the right amount of shade.

Trees throw off different types of shadows. Tall columnar trees provide a striking vertical accent in the garden but send out only a thin sliver of shade. A round-headed Japanese maple creates a mound of shade, although the fine leaves let light filter through. A large-leaved maple makes a large shadow and the more substantial leaves make a denser shadow. Find out as much as you can about a tree's habit and requirements before you make your decision.

Planting trees and shrubs for shade is a long-term strategy, for it takes years for even the fastest growing shrub or tree to stretch out to a height to effectively provide shade. Yet trees are the aristocrats of the garden, and shrubs bring blooms and form to the garden. Both are truly worth waiting for.

Deciduous trees let winter sun peep through windows to warm a house's interior, while in summer leaves block the sun from driving up house temperatures. Carefully chosen fruit trees can bring the pleasures of fresh fruit to the kitchen in the time it takes to walk from the garden to the house. The fragrance of some flowering trees brings another dimension to the garden.

Yet, living so closely with trees, you must check out their

Variegated shrubs and trees have a way of brightening up an area and calling attention to themselves.

Some shrubs grow very thick and cast a deeper shade.

PRUNING TO MODIFY SHADE

Removing just a few branches on a tree can make a dramatic difference in the amount of shade a tree casts.

Consult your gardening plan (see page 29) to measure out the major areas of shade in the garden underneath trees or shrubs. Any areas with Shade 3 or 4 should be investigated to see if the heavy shade can be lightened with pruning. However, some trees do not lend themselves to altering. Columnar cedars or evergreens that grow in Christmas-tree shapes cannot be successfully pruned, or at least not in any way that adds beauty to the garden. Pruning these types only destroys the natural shape of the tree and leaves an ugly result. Most other trees and large shrubs can be pruned to allow light to filter in to plants underneath.

Although late winter or early spring is the usual time for heavy pruning of deciduous plants, you can lightly prune all year round without injuring a plant. Some evergreen shrubs and climbers are pruned after blooming, for if blossoms are borne on wood produced the last season, pruning in late winter would take off the blooms. Make sure to research the appropriate time to prune for a specific plant.

Pruning Basics

Pruning need not be daunting—it simply shapes the plant to form a framework for healthy growth. If you feel nervous, comfort yourself with the fact that, as with many endeavors, you only improve with practice. There is also comfort in the fact that under-

pruning does less damage to most plants than overpruning.

Measure the eventual mature size of a plant against the site where you intend to plant it. This will simplify pruning decisions and chores. Hoping that a standard tree grows slowly in a small space is planning for extra work in the future. Select the appropriate size plant to fit your space.

A few general maxims can guide both the novice and the casual expert through the pruning process, and they are applicable to most horticultural situations.

Simple Pruning Know-How

• Prune off dead, dying, diseased or cracked and

Different trees are best pruned at different times of the year depending on disease resistance, bloom time and other factors. Know what the best time is for your trees before grabbing your pruning saw!

broken branches to discourage the spread of disease or insect infestation through rotting wood.
- Take out branches that cross through the center of the tree from one side of the tree to the other. Prune branches that rub on each other, scarring the bark and leaving open wounds that encourage insect infestation.

- Cut out rooted suckers (sprouts that grow out of the ground from the roots) or vertical-growing water sprouts (fast-growing sprouts that shoot straight upward).
- Prune to an outward-facing bud for a compact framework of branches less likely to break. Also called "heading back branches," this means pruning to a bud that as it

matures will point directly out of the center of the tree, not growing across branches or into the tree's center.

To simplify the process, realize that you can, and often should, prune your plants all year long; rid yourself of the notion of once-a-year exhaustive pruning sessions just before the plants leaf out or start their spring growth. Winter pruning when plants are dormant allows you to see the plant's overall skeleton so you can make adjustments to the plant's form. However winter pruning spurs vigorous growth of water sprouts. Mid- to late-summer pruning should be less rigorous but the plant's response will also be less vigorous, without the excessive growth that occurs in the spring.

Thinning and Heading Cuts

There are two kinds of pruning cuts. *Thinning cuts* trim branches back to the central trunk to make a compact frame. *Heading cuts* trim back to a bud or a branch to shorten the main

Heading cuts

Thinning cuts

Heading and thinning cuts change the look of trees and shrubs in different ways. Consider the look you want before pruning.

STRATEGIES FOR MODIFYING SHADE

1. Use heading and thinning cuts to prune appropriate shrubs and trees to let in more light.
2. Plant appropriate shrubs and trees that can be pruned to create a high canopy.
3. Take out trees that crowd structures or fences.
4. Design and build a shade structure, either a fence, lath house, pergola, arbor, gazebo or garden pavilion.
5. Use vines to quickly cover a structure.

When pruning hedges, leave the bottom slightly wider than the top to allow more light to filter in to the middle of the hedge.

branch and aim the new, emerging growth in the direction you feel benefits the overall shape. Regardless of the type of cut, make sure your tools are as sharp as possible to avoid tearing the bark or leaving splintered cuts that make the plant vulnerable to insect penetration. Hardware stores often offer inexpensive sharpening services, or you can use a whetstone to keep your tools in top condition.

Use a tool appropriate to the diameter of the branch. Hand pruners trim branches with a diameter of up to ³/₄ inch. Racheting clippers help gardeners with less hand strength cut through small branches. Loppers cut branches up to 2 inches thick while saws can tackle branches 2 to 3 inches in diameter. Straining to cut a branch larger than a tool's capability can dull the blade or throw the tool out of alignment. Often, such cuts end up savaging the branch, leaving it splintered and rough—thus vulnerable to invasion from wood-eating insects.

Perform thinning cuts on trees, particularly when taking out large branches, in three stages. First, cut a heavy branch halfway back to the trunk. Then make a second cut halfway between the first cut and the trunk. Make the third cut to avoid a heavy limb tearing off before the cut is complete. The position of the cut is important to avoid excess injury to the plant. Every branch has a curl or ripple of bark just where it joins the main trunk. This curl, called the branch collar, contains chemicals that naturally inhibit rot. If you cut a branch flat against the trunk, you remove the collar and its disease-fighting abilities. Cut off the branch about ¹/₂ inch away from the collar and at an angle with the closest edge at the top of the cut (see diagram). This allows rain to run off, and prevents it from puddling within the cut to rot the wood.

Terminal Buds and Lateral Buds

All plant growth occurs in the terminal buds and lateral buds. The terminal buds, at the tips of the branches, cause the stem to grow in length. The lateral buds grow along the sides of the stem and produce sideways growth, called lateral growth or just laterals. The terminal buds produce a hormone that inhibits the growth of lateral buds. When you prune a terminal bud, you stop the growth of the stem and encourage the growth of lateral buds, which may consequently grow out to become terminal buds. There are also dormant buds, visible bumps on the branches that may be stimulated into growth through proper pruning.

Water sprouts and suckers are two types of growth that must be pruned out; otherwise they will drain the tree's resources while looking unsightly as well. Water sprouts grow up vertically from the trunk or branch, sometimes as a response to winter pruning. Prune these. But if there are many of them growing in response to a winter pruning, wait until *late* summer to take them all out; summer pruning retards their growth.

The tarlike salves that are said to speed the healing of pruning cuts actually retard healing. In fact, they may leave the plant even more vulnerable to rot and insects and should not be used.

Avoid cutting too deep when you prune—the branch collar is important for protecting the tree.

The Japanese Maple

Japanese maples are among the most favored trees in a small garden. Their near perfect proportions of size, delicate leaves and lovely leaf colors—from deep purples to light greens—means there is a tree for nearly every garden. There are so many varieties and cultivars that there are nurseries and catalogs that only feature Japanese maples.

Height: to 30 feet
Leaf colors: Light chartreuse green, purples, variegated

*Privet (*Ligustrum *spp.), pruned up to the topmost branches, makes an unusual shade canopy for an arbor. The sculptural effect of the bare branches adds to the structure's interest while functioning to block the sun.*

A good cut at the right time of year is the best prescription.

Pruning Mature Trees

Pruning large, overgrown trees may be too much for the gardener with only a pruning saw and clippers. In these cases, you should call in an arborist with professional equipment to do the job. Consider the fact that summer pruning may be more useful on mature trees than winter pruning, for it does not encourage the wealth of growth that results after winter pruning. Consult with an arborist before making your decision. A professional arborist is certified, bonded, licensed, insured and accustomed to consulting on trees, both for hazards to the health of the tree and the surrounding area.

If you decide to work on a tree, take your time. A tree neglected for several years may need a number of pruning sessions to gradually bring it back to trim. Be cautious: Over-pruning the first year can let so much light into the interior that the tree will develop sunscald. The first winter, prune off some of the too-large branches to bring light into the canopy; use heading cuts to shorten the limbs. Cut out any dead or crossing wood. Then, in late summer, prune out the excess growth from the winter pruning and continue to shape the tree. Gradually prune back the branches and lower the canopy. Continue the pruning regime the next several years, gradually restoring the tree to a graceful and purposeful shape.

Vines

Annual vines need no pruning, just some direction to keep them from growing so closely that they limit air circulation, which encourages the mildew diseases to which they are susceptible.

Prune perennial vines to encourage new fruit or flowering wood, which grows on old wood in some plants and on new wood in others. Make sure to determine the growth pattern of the vine before you prune so you do not sacrifice blooms.

Pruning smaller trees can make a fabulous dappled shade—perfect for many shade-loving plants.

« CHAPTER 3 »
GARDEN STYLE

Nature's forests, hills and meadows have their own natural beauty, but humankind has never been willing to leave it alone.

Gardeners and landscape designers from the beginning of time have wanted to manage the green horizon, moving a plant here or there, taking out a tree to obtain a long view or digging out a hill to make a pond. Garden historians, anthropologists and archeologists have uncovered a great deal of information about humans' earliest efforts to tame and arrange nature, but most of us know little about it. When we look at our shade gardens to make improvements, an understanding of the long history of gardens can help increase success and clarify the design concept.

Then it's time to choose a style that suits your *own* personal taste.

NEW PLANTS FOR THE GARDEN

Many plants native to North America became European favorites, and only then gained popularity on this side of the Atlantic.

The adventures of the early European explorers traveling perilously around the globe in tiny wooden boats is matched by the daring feats of plant explorers to discover rare or unknown species—climbing to the tops of jungle canopies to find orchids or trudging through swamps filled with toothed creatures. Any remarkable discovery was followed by anxious months, tending to specimens regardless of the lurching of a ship on wild seas, of freezing cold or lack of fresh water when surrounded by salty seas. Fortunes were won and lost with the importation of new plants and with the development of new planting styles ... a history as complete with intrigue, greed, trust and mistrust as any story of gold digging in the American West.

Yet discussions of garden design bring a glazed eye to the most experienced gardeners, who love the plants, the daily tending and nurturing, but cannot be bothered with the historical underpinnings of why we think a garden looks beautiful. Yet when we go to design or redesign our shade garden, a basic understanding of garden design will bring about more satisfying results for all the hard work and expense.

Learning the History of Plants

Garden design—the result of culture, philosophy, art and nature—can be documented from earliest times. Garden style evolved from this long tradition of arranging plants and trees in certain patterns which were

found pleasing for various reasons. For example, in certain religious orders, herbs or plants with symbolic meaning functioned within a design that noted their importance. Plants arranged in circles and squares in both Islamic architecture and European gardens represented the cosmos, humankind's work inspired by the heavens and divinity. As artists learned about the art of perspective, the garden designers incorporated their principles to alter the perspective of the garden. In time, certain trends became classic, repeated time and time again through the centuries. Although you may not know why raised beds seem appealing, or why every house needs patches of lawn, those aspects of garden design have historic roots, as well.

This garden creatively uses squares of pachysandra and sheared boxwood to create a pleasing walkway to the house. The boxwood pruned into balls adds whimsy to the otherwise quite formal design.

Creating a Designed Garden

A designed garden is within the reach of every gardener; in fact, many gardeners design intuitively, without realizing or recognizing the design principles they are using. There is a subtle sense of mastery in a planned garden—the difference between the abstract art of a kindergartener (wild and free with bold color), and a professional artist, whose painting has order and a discipline that causes the onlooker to feel as if a window has been opened to look through on purpose. Quality garden design, known in the trade as the "good bones" of a garden, organizes space and then arranges color, pattern and movement with unity and balance of all the elements for a totally conceived composition.

Understanding the different garden styles gives the gardener a template with which to look at his or her gardens. Knowing the history of garden design is simply increasing the ways we can consider organizing plants. We are also influenced by climate and the specific site of our own gardens. Never be afraid to interpret these styles in your own way, for a garden is a work of art, and art must always be a personal expression.

Planning for Garden Use

Planning doesn't need to be overwhelming. As a way of assessing your garden design, walk through it with a clipboard and a piece of paper to sketch a map.

First, place the major structures. Set down the borders of the garden, the pathways and the open areas. Use circles or rectangles scaled to size to designate trees, shrubs and flower beds. Identify the shade areas by cross-hatching from light to dark the light shade (Shade 1 to 2), medium shade (Shade 3) and heavy shade (Shade 4). Looking at the map, consider your needs for the garden. Do you want areas for barbecues, display beds for favorite plants, a water garden, raised planters for fruits and vegetables? Ask yourself if you want:

- Entertaining space
- More intensive gardening areas
- Active areas for kids and family for games such as croquet or volleyball
- Increased shade areas from structures

Depending upon your assessment, you may decide to redo your garden, calling on the services of a landscape architect or garden designer once you determine your own personal goals. Many gardeners decide a complete remodeling is out of the question. Yet within the garden, subtle changes can transform what was ordinary into an attractive outdoor living room. Consider covering a patio, replanting a border in green and white, planting a hedge to wall off a garden room, adding raised beds for fruits and vegetables or creating a barbecue area underneath a tree shaded too densely for lawn. Any of these projects make a difference in your garden.

These changes should take place within a unifying design, however. In your house, you would never tack on a roof with a modern "A" frame next to a Victorian gable or a log cabin, so your garden changes should take place within a context of a general design.

As a starting point in thinking about your garden design, consider three different garden styles, those of the formal garden, the naturalistic garden and the Japanese-style garden. Once you understand these styles, you can consider just what kind of changes you want to make to your garden.

A Japanese-style garden often uses water to reflect the sky.

THE FORMAL GARDEN

Anyone familiar with the European garden tradition has experienced the design of a formal garden in their city square, in public gardens laid out just like the lines of a French château garden, or in rose gardens with great square beds sometimes edged with low green lines of boxwood or woody perennials. The formal garden design repeats forms and shapes with mathematical regularity. All shapes are symmetrical, most often with sharp angles and straight lines forming geometrical patterns but sometimes using ovals or circles. Important to the whole scheme is proportion and balance, so the dimensions of the walkways, paths and beds are measured out in relation to the available space. Often the garden includes hedges pruned to perfection and topiary forms in squares or cones.

History

This careful planning harkens back to the aesthetics of the grand European cathedrals of the medieval period, with their regular parade of columns along the side aisles, or even earlier in the Greek and Roman temples and earlier yet, the sacred buildings of the Egyptians. Garden design mimicked architecture with colonnades of cedars along walkways or enclosing garden rooms.

Straight lines dominate in formal gardens.

In Coimbra, Italy, the garden of Septimius Severus (146 to 211 A.D.) looks like a contemporary city garden with raised beds around a central pool. The garden's geometric form presents a unifying theme, particularly when echoed with plantings and

Formal parterres *(see p. 31) divide the garden into neat geometric shapes. The boxwood* (Buxus *spp.) grows slowly but successfully in shade. Although some yearly pruning is necessary to keep it shaped, its crisp and trim look tidies a garden.*

The overflowing mounds of the shade-loving impatiens soften the formal geometric lines of this garden with its large pool.

seating as a destination after a stroll through the garden adds to the pleasure of garden viewing. Although in the large formal gardens this strolling might take several hours, the concept translated to a small garden works ideally for entryways or garden areas that are pathways to other parts of the garden.

In small spaces and particularly tiny entry gardens off the front sidewalk, a formal garden with clipped hedges and a neat walkway seems a welcome relief from the chaos of the outside world. Although the spareness from the clean lines might be too prim for some, plants can soften the lines of pathways by foaming over the edges.

Maintenance

Although not without upkeep—the hedging material must be trimmed regularly and the paths swept or raked, if using gravel, to keep them tidy—the formal garden can be simple to maintain because the incisive design gives an appearance of neatness with its clean lines. The discipline of a simple, formal garden can be equal to that of the minimalist Japanese-style garden, and the results of both are the pleasure of uncluttered lines and classic beauty.

structures. The viewer's eye is led through the space, and the regularity of design functions to relax and please the senses in its comfortable balance.

One of the most interesting formal gardens is in France, at Villandry. There the parterres—square or rectangle planting beds hedged with clipped boxwood—are filled with vegetables, as was customary in the 18th century. The château gardens were not only designed to present beauty, but they also supplied the kitchen

with fresh produce. This garden is a good example of the versatility of the formal garden, for it can serve the function of beauty as well as practicality.

Modern Formal Gardens

In contemporary gardens, we have adapted the formal garden precepts to our raised planter beds, the wood of the bed edging representing the hedging of the classical garden. Low-maintenance plants within the boxes can provide a simple green filling throughout the year, or they can, as in Villandry, be used for the kitchen garden, filled with flowers for cutting or even planted as an herb garden.

The formal garden was meant for strolling, for walking around on paths while gazing at the plants in the gardens. Planning the garden to include

Boxwood hedges, even though not pruned in stiff right angles, still add structure to the formal garden.

The pathway's straight edge lines are picked up by the border of gray lamb's-ear. Imagine the scene without the concrete pillars; their form spotlights the start of the path. The pillars add architectural detail, an important element of the formal garden.

THE NATURAL GARDEN

Contrary to the formal garden, the natural garden avoids straight lines and sharp crisp angles. Instead it imitates nature, with softly undulating lines, gentle curves and an asymmetrical organization. Natural gardens developed as a reaction to severely formal gardens. There are a number of different steps in the evolution of the natural garden, starting out with 19th-century British garden designers such as Gertrude Jekyll and William Robinson, the author of *The Wild Garden*, published in 1870.

History

Jekyll began to imitate the humble English cottagers at the end of the Victorian era who, with no great expectations, planted their gardens with a variety of different, cheerfully blooming plants. No straight lines, no enclosing boxwood hedges—just plants along the walkway to the front door blooming in splashes of color, form and texture. Instead of the formal geometrically designed beds of tender bedding plants so loved by the Victorians, Robinson introduced informal borders that mixed bulbs, perennials and annuals.

In America at the end of the 19th century, famed landscape architect Frederick Law Olmsted, the designer of Central Park in New York City, was commissioned to plan the gardens for Biltmore House, the 125,000-acre estate of George Washington Vanderbilt. His design included a number of gardens around the house which became increasingly naturalistic as they spread out to the surrounding woods. His use of rhododendrons, azaleas and dogwood makes the now-public park legendary in the spring.

In the next 50 years, formal gardens continued to dominate, albeit with a loosened sense of formality. But today, with an increasing interest in native plants, more and more gardeners are plowing up lawns and pulling out trimmed hedges to sow wildflower meadows. As more gardeners live in cities with less access to wild places, turning a sedate backyard garden into a miniature woodland has its appeal. We all need a bit of wilderness in our lives.

Modern Natural Gardens

Interestingly, the same principles apply to planning a natural garden as well as a formal garden. Why? Because plants should never be set in helter-skelter but with a sense of order and design. Assess the space you are planting and choose your plants according to their mature

This carefully planted creekside imitates the forest's end at a meadow stream. Although it looks unplanned, the gardener planted azaleas and camelias for spring color.

Plantings along a shady stream add a variety of textures and forms.

A grass path leads the garden stroller past a mounded bed with plants graduated from low in the foreground to taller in the background.

size, color, shape and relationship to the plants neighboring them. Planning a naturalistic shade garden means you must additionally take into account the amount of shade the plants require. Remember that nature doesn't have nurseries to go to; consequently, the types of plants in a naturalistic setting are actually quite few.

Repeating a few plants through an area mimics nature more authentically than a spattering of many different plants. The larger the area, the more types of plants you can use. But clustering similar plants produces a better effect than stringing them out or spotting them here or there. An odd number of plants in a cluster looks better to the eye than an even tally.

The design of a naturalistic garden fits almost any situation. A small front entry garden or just a portion of a back garden can be converted to a woodland garden easily. Even a lawn leading to the area can look like a grassy meadow when crocuses are planted within it to bloom in the early spring. Unless you want to replant the bulbs every fall, after the crocuses bloom, let the grass grow until the crocus leaves begin to yellow—it won't take long. If you must mow, do not

trim the lawn sharply, but mow it at the highest setting possible, mowing around the bulbs until the leaves start to die back.

Bulbs make reliable additions to the woodland garden. When adding bulbs, plant them in groups of five or more, spacing them in the planting hole with room around each one. Stagger the clumps irregularly. Remember that daffodils, snowdrops and other early spring bulbs naturalize splendidly under deciduous trees, blooming before

The natural aspect of the plants spilling onto one another makes this garden seem a wild place although the plant choices have been made with care.

the trees leaf out and spreading to make larger and larger clumps the following years. As with the crocus in the lawn, do not cut back the green leaves until they wither and yellow; this will ensure the next year's bloom.

Maintenance

Part of the authenticity of a natural garden is the look of the forest floor. Mulching the natural garden mimics the duff—the mixture of dried leaves composting in a wild forest—with the added benefit of minimizing garden upkeep. Mulch minimizes the need to water, and when 3 to 5 inches thick, discourages seeds from germinating. Mulching your woodland beds keeps the soil cool, just how the shade plants like it, and also maintains the soil in the acidic range, which is preferable for most shade plants. The woodland garden is the original low-maintenance garden. (If this type of garden interests you, see pages 40-43 in the "Collection of Shade Gardens" section for more discussion.)

THE JAPANESE-STYLE GARDEN

In 1853 President Millard Fillmore sent Admiral Matthew Perry to threaten such a forceful invasion of Japan that the Japanese agreed to a treaty to open their ports to American ships and to initiate trade. Before the Japanese signed the treaty in 1854, they had shunned all outside trade or influence, allowing the world's trading nations access to only one port, and prohibiting travel to any other parts of the island. That treaty and the subsequent opening of Japan revealed what had been an unknown world to outsiders. In particular, travelers discovered a wealth of plants that the Japanese had brought back from other parts of Asia and improved

through centuries of cultivation and cross-breeding, not to mention the stunningly different aesthetic of their lovely gardens.

History

Unlike the European formal gardens, with beds laid out in geometric precision and inlaid with a superfluity of plants, the Japanese gardens were spare, often using only a few well-chosen plants (sometimes pruned or bonsaied), and elements of rocks, gravel or moss. Adapted from earlier Chinese gardens, 19th-century Japanese gardens were based on a blending of Shinto and Buddhist religious beliefs—namely that after life, the human spirit might be incorporated into natural things, like rocks or trees, making natural objects as important as humans. Gardens were considered spiritual places, important to the well-being of the whole person, not just a recreational outlet. Religious shrines, monasteries and private houses celebrated the importance of the garden as a part of daily spiritual activity.

Although Americans and Europeans did not totally comprehend the religious and spiritual significance of the Japanese gardens, they were impressed with the purity of the aesthetics. So impressed were they with this new style, that Europeans hired and transported Japanese gardeners to set up gardens in their homelands. In Scotland, at Crowden, a Japanese garden was commissioned to be built in 1907 by Taki Honda, who went there from Japan to transform a boggy field into a garden. In his garden at Giverny, the famous French painter Claude Monet created a Japanese garden and

A woven bamboo screen joins the two buildings together while making a stage for the gravel and rocks. Without the screen, the drama of the gravel and rock would be lost into the foliage blocked by the screen.

built a bridge based on the picture of one in a woodblock print he owned. The Japanese bridge stars innumerable times in his justly famous lily pond paintings.

Modern Japanese-Style Gardens

As Westerners today, we still have difficulty following the strict rules of the traditional Japanese garden makers, with their code of regulations such as not placing mountain rocks near water. Even so, gardeners find the precise sensibility of balance and proportion a worthy challenge to carry out in their gardens. The calm beauty of a Japanese-style garden comes from the simplicity of design, with a minimum of elements and often highlighted by the placement of one or two rocks, the use of gravel in swirling patterns and moss or grasses. The gardens in Japanese monasteries

The carefully laid rocky beach—with the iron heron sculpture, the rock-lined shore and the bridge—are all elements that give this garden a sense of Japanese style. Although the planting is not strictly in the style of a classical Japanese garden, the different elements tie the composition together.

The view of the landscape has been carefully composed to be viewed in the frame of the doorway.

On the other side of the doorway, you can see how carefully the garden has been designed to relate to the architecture of the door. The door frames the gentle angle of the rock wall.

were objects for contemplation, so designers created spiritual metaphors with their elements. Rocks, for example, within swept gravel, looked like a mountain rising out of the sea. A monastic disciple might contemplate life within the representation of swirling waters and the force of the immutable mountain.

Many Japanese gardens focus on walkways of large stepping-stones leading the way to the teahouse where the important social ritual of taking tea was performed. In contemporary gardens, the pathway might be subtly refined to create an ocean-like scene with the planting of a moss groundcover or other low-growing plants around stepping-stones leading to a seating area.

Gardens in Japan were designed to be viewed from inside the houses, with subtle use of perspective and proportion to enlarge the view (home gardens are often very small in size in Japan). Large plants were set in the foreground of the design with smaller, lower growing plants at the back—a trick to make the eye think there is more depth to the garden than actually exists. Although you may not need to effect this trick perspective, take to heart the importance of designing the garden from a particular point of view, whether it is just as you walk inside the front gate, from a dining room window, or seated at the very back of the garden.

A water feature with fish is an important element in Japanese gardens. A low bowl set into the ground with a single waterlily, or a small reflection pond made from a plastic liner (see page 62 for details on working with a liner) reflects the sky and adds the movement of birds and insects to the garden—all important elements to the Japanese gardener. Regardless of the size of your water garden, make sure to add a

Rocks and gravel may be the ultimate solution in situations where grass or plants are unsuccessful, either because of lack of water or light. Yet, as you can see in this scene, the drama of rocks and swept gravel presents anything but a boring view.

to keep the proportions appropriate to the space.

Like the fine simplicity of Shaker furniture designs, with no fancy trimmings, the Japanese-style garden's very simplicity is the heart of its sophistication. You'll find after living with a Japanese garden that, on reflection, it seems very full. (If this type of garden interests you, see pages 44-47 in the "Collection of Shade Gardens" section for more discussion.)

few fish. Be advised, however, that even the smallest amount of water becomes a breeding ground for mosquitoes; goldfish or mosquito fish gobble the larva.

The aesthetics of a Japanese-style garden are based on absence, not presence, so work with only a few elements of plants, rocks, water and gravel. Plants should be repeated so the view seems unified. Bamboo, plentiful in Japan when lumber from trees was not, is a common material in fencing. Large stones are set to present the most impressive side to the view, but should not be overly obscured by plant matter. Use moss or low-growing grasses around the rocks.

sure to keep them clear of debris. Prune trees and shrubs

Maintenance

The simplicity of the Japanese-style garden makes it easy to maintain. The lack of complicated plantings and use of perennials, shrubs and trees simplifies maintenance.

However, the gardener must tidy by weeding, sweeping and trimming to keep all the elements in balance. If moss or low groundcovers are used, make

A useful solution to difficult growing situations—bonsai trees sit dramatically within a sea of gravel. The pots allow the gardener to move them after a period of display. Flowering seasonal shrubs would look equally as elegant and spare.

CHAPTER 4

A COLLECTION OF SHADE GARDENS

Most of us fall into a garden already created by another person. Sometimes we are lucky enough to inherit a carefully designed and planted garden. But more often we have a random collection of every previous gardeners' favorite plants set in where they thrived and spread indiscriminately. Sorting out what you want is essential to create the garden that gives you the most pleasure.

The following examples of the main styles of gardening should help you look at your own shade garden and begin to catalog its best features. Remember though, that you can pick and choose elements of these gardens to transplant to your own. You may have an isolated side space perfect for a Japanese-style garden or your front entry may call out for a woodland planting. Be wary of mixing too many styles; a cohesive visual frame is more satisfying than bits of this and that.

THE WOODLAND GARDEN

What could be more refreshing at the end of a hectic day than walking along a shady path through the woods? You note the variety of plants, the beauty of their textured leaves and enjoy the sudden burst of wildflower blooms tucked here and there.

Flowering bulbs surprise you in all seasons. Spring daffodils and species tulips pop up for weeks and camassia naturalizes to make drifts of long-lasting blue blossoms. In summer, swaying lilies bloom 5 feet high. In the fall, waves of the pinkish-purple

blossoms of autumn crocus (*Colchicum* spp.) resemble water lilies as their blooms break through the ground. Flowering shrubs mark the seasons with blooms and leaf color under the protecting umbrella of the taller trees. Although it looks like it

When you decide upon a woodland garden, draw your inspiration from nature.

planted itself, a natural garden grows by design.

Bringing the Woods Home

A backyard woodland garden imitates nature's design with a natural style in which the plants seem to jostle and compete with each other. In actuality, the plantings of a woodland garden must be carefully selected and arranged. The good thing is that you don't need acres and acres to transform into a woodland scene: Even the back of a small garden can be transformed into a woodland with just a winding path and an appropriate planting style. A front entry garden presents a fine showing as a woodland garden, creating privacy by screening off roads and sidewalks, making the transition from public street to private oasis.

Choosing Your Plants

Take the opportunity to study natural woodland gardens or the gardens of friends in your

The mowed grassy path through the garden is a clever way to imitate a meadow yet provide the structure of a pathway. Letting the lawn grow long in the spring allows the gardener to plant early, low-growing drifts of bulbs such as tiny daffodils, grape hyacinths or crocus. After the leaves begin to yellow, you can mow the lawn without jeopardizing next year's bloom.

This planting scheme of birches with low groundcover could be easily adapted to a front garden entry or a small side-yard garden.

area to discover the kinds of plantings, the design of the paths and any shade structures you want to build in your own garden. As an easy first step in starting a list of desired plants, visualize your woodland as three heights.

First there's the canopy of tall trees. Next shrubs and smaller understory trees reach up to clothe the upper spaces. Then shorter shrubs, annuals and perennials hug the ground. Keeping in mind the three levels you want to fill, choose your plants according to their mature heights.

To provide visual interest, vary the leaf texture of your plant collection, juxtaposing a large-leafed plant just above a groundcover with thin or finely cut leaves. To provide accents, look for mounding shrubs, use upright grasses for vertical accents and choose variegated, colored or golden-leafed plants. When choosing plants for a woodland garden, look for wilder plants—no pruned boxwood or daffodils in rows.

The Year-Round Garden

In a woodland garden, the seasons are particularly apparent so plan for periods of seasonal interest in the garden. In winter, when many trees are dormant and leafless, there is a particular wonder to shrubs and trees with brightly colored bark such as the dogwoods and the birches. Certain of the Japanese maples have bright red bark that lights up a dull winter palette of grays and white. Many early spring shrubs such as witch hazel, forsythia and flowering quince bloom with dramatic bright

This adaptation of a woodland garden uses azaleas to soften the rigid effect of trees planted in rows. The shrubs effectively mimic the woodland look with a stylish sparseness.

Although the trees are planted symmetrically, the curving path softens and naturalizes the garden.

Carefully chosen plants provide variety in the woodland garden. The range of tones from gray to chartreuse green makes interesting viewing. Note how the light gray pops out from the greens, especially against the dark green backdrop.

to bloom from early spring through the first days of summer in a shady garden. There are also deciduous azaleas accustomed to cold weather that bloom out in spring in oranges and sun-bright yellow colors as well as the range of pinks and purples.

In summer, you can have hummingbird-beloved blooms from honeysuckle used as a groundcover or climbing on a boundary fence. There are even autumn crocuses with pinky purple blooms.

Don't neglect the other seasons; with research, you will find something that can produce interest—blooms, brightly colored foliage or even berries—through every season of the year. The goal is for your woodland garden to have a focus at each time of the year.

Planning the Garden

Once you have a sense of your plantings, you must lay out your garden. Start by drawing it out on paper. Regardless of whether you are digging up lawn to create your garden or interplanting with establishing trees and shrubs, draw a garden map with circles indicating existing plantings and the quality of their shade. (See map-making discussion, page 29).

A map makes it easier to lay out a path. A gentle meandering path that ambles along through the trees and plants is one of the most charming aspects of a

blossoms on bare stems, making wild splashes of color.

Early spring is also the time to take particular advantage of the sun that still streams into the areas underneath the leafless trees. Spring bulbs light up the ground underneath deciduous trees before bursting out in their spring display of bright green leaves. Among all the

hybrid bulbs are some types which naturalize well, spreading each year to become great drifts of color year after year. In particular daffodils, species tulips, leucojum and grape hyacinths are standbys which return as regularly as the robins.

Choose rhododendrons and azaleas, suited to almost any climate, in a variety of cultivars natural garden. Try to end the path in a seating area, a destination complete with a gallery of special plants in form or fragrance or an interesting collection of annuals or perennials in containers.

Paths

Maintaining a path free of weeds can be difficult. A simple dirt path mulched heavily with bark or partially decomposed chippings stays weed free when you place impenetrable barriers underneath the mulch. For barriers you can use recyclable materials such as cardboard or sections of newspaper. Although they break down over the course of several seasons, most of the weed seeds will have germinated and died by that time and will no longer be a problem. Commercially produced weed barriers are also effective. More permanent paths such as bricks, paving stones or concrete should be edged with plants to create the softer, more natural look of the woods.

Once the path has been established, you can start on

This round pond bridges the two styles of formal and woodland. It makes a transition to the wild forest beyond.

the planting areas. Make sure to work in generous quantities of compost and other soil amendments. When you first set in your chosen plants, the landscape may look somewhat bare. Plant annuals or wildflowers around the perennials and shrubs to fill in the spaces until the permanent plantings

have a chance to grow. When adding wildflowers to your planting, choose a mixture collected specifically for your location and designed for shade planting. If you plant wildflowers, you won't be able to spread a heavy mulch until after they have bloomed. In wildflower patches, mulch with only about $1/4$ to $1/2$ inch of cover.

When the planting is completed, mulch heavily with 3 to 4 inches of compost to keep weeds down, maintain moisture and keep the soil friable. Maintain an irrigation schedule as necessary. Carefully nurture your woodland planting as you would a formal garden. Make sure to fertilize the garden in the fall in cold weather areas or the spring in warm climate regions to ensure continued healthy growth.

The meandering path, carving its way through rhododendrons and azaleas, has been mulched to keep it weed-free and natural looking. The plantings have been grouped together to imitate a woodland—with low ferns, medium-height azaleas and tall rhododendrons crowding together under the canopy trees.

Moss, Grasses, Gravel and Stones

Although moss, grasses, gravel and stones are landscape elements traditionally associated with Japanese-style gardens, they also have a place in contemporary shade gardens. A pared-away contemporary landscape offers the repose of simplicity with the added attraction of being low-maintenance. In shade gardens, using these ingredients can be a practical solution for areas with low light levels that ordinarily grow only crops of unsightly weeds or dense growths of ivy. Whether the area is a tiny cut-out on the north side of a city lot, a dark entry garden or a small patch of back garden surrounded by skyscrapers, you can carve out a successful garden using moss, grasses, gravel and stones.

Although seemingly simple in its arrangements, a moss garden needs careful attention to the aesthetics of each of the elements and how it affects the overall composition or design. The texture of gravel offsets the simple tailored look of the moss. Shade-tolerant grasses, particularly variegated grasses, can be used to great advantage as bursts of texture and color in the otherwise serene setting. Small tufts of grass fringed around rocks appear almost as if an ocean wave were bursting against its shore.

Moss cloaks the narrow paving stone stairway.

Planning the Garden

Consider your site carefully, for the trickiest part of this garden is working out the balance in the design. The impact of many flowering plants is out of place in this garden. Draw out your garden map, checking the areas of shade and noting the boundaries of the area you are working with. Gravel can be used as a path or around a path of large flat steppingstones. Smaller pea gravel feels more comfortable for walking on, while a larger gravel can be spread as a stronger design element. Large rocks may be difficult to transport into cramped areas; in these situations, build a rock formation with multiple

rocks just large enough to conveniently transport on a dolly.

Points of Focus in the Garden

The traditional Japanese garden was meant to be viewed
from specific angles—a focus
employed by landscape archi-
tects but often forgotten by
home gardeners. Whether your
moss/grass garden is in the
Japanese style or not, place the
elements in the most effective
sites. To do this, check the garden's main vantage points both
from the indoors and the ex-
terior views. Stand at each
spot, whether it be through the
living room window or from a
pathway to the front door.
Plan the placement of rocks,
grasses and gravel with these
viewpoints in mind for the
most dramatic focal points of
the garden. A cardboard box in
the approximate size of the
rocks and plants in containers
can help you visualize—with a
stretch of the imagination—the
balance of your design.
Remember: Keeping the design
extremely simple with only a
few elements gives a more dramatic effect.

Using gravel in the deepest shade areas and a lawn of moss solves the problem of how to garden in deep shade. The soft shape of pachysandra, which grows successfully in low light, gives a tidy appearance to the garden.

Grasses provide upright
movement as well as color and
texture to the garden. But
choose the variety carefully, for
if used in conjunction with a
moss lawn, an invasive grass
can overrun the moss and
become a weedy menace.

Varieties of carex, a well-
behaved grass, come in sizes
from 6 inches to 24 inches tall
and in a range of foliage color
from sea green to creamy white
and green, to blue-gray and
even rusty brown. Festuca

The shade under the high canopy trees is too dense to make a grass lawn possible. Yet this stunning moss lawn is just as effective.

Bricks with moss grown in between.

GROWING GRASS IN THE SHADE

If you want to grow turfgrass in the shade, you should first determine if the area you have in mind receives at least 4 hours of sun a day. You can prune tree limbs up to 8 or 10 feet above the ground to bring in more light. Without this amount of light, grass will not be able to grow and you should use a groundcover instead.

Choose the right turf for the situation. Some grasses are more shade tolerant than others. In warm areas, St Augustine, centipedegrass and zoysiagrass work better than other types. In cool-season areas, try fine fescue, bentgrass, rough bluegrass or tall fescue. Check with local experts for their favorites.

To care for your grass, water deeply early in the morning, enough to have the water pene-
trate at least 5 to 8 inches deep. When mowing, leave the grass longer—at least $2^1/4$ to 3 inches high. Longer leaves will absorb more light. Only use half the amount of fertilizer recommended.

Avoid any heavy use of the grass which will tear up the root structure that is already fragile from the less-than-perfect growing environment.

Pruning the lower branches of shrubs and trees allows more light into the garden and presents a sculptural effect. The gravel makes an effective groundcover in deep shade.

species, little blue-green or silver-gray tufts, can take shade and are durable in a low-maintenance garden. If you want a bit of seasonal color in your scheme, consider interplanting a variegated iris among a variegated grass. The foliage forms are alike enough not to distract and you have the added pleasure of iris blooms in spring.

Moss Plantings

Incorporating moss into your garden design offers an extremely practical solution to a low-light situation. Moss succeeds under trees that cast shade too deep for a grass lawn. Moss in conjunction with a serene arrangement of rocks and gravel adds a touch of green that softens the effect of the design while unifying the whole with its flat texture.

However, consider these aspects of a moss garden. Although moss requires little light to look its best, it does need constant moisture to maintain its green. It is essential to maintain a strict weeding schedule to keep moss from being overrun by pesky weeds, particularly when you first start the moss lawn.

Many gardeners already have moss growing in the area they would like to convert to a moss garden. Having observed the moss winning out over the lawn these gardeners decide to "join 'em, not fight 'em." If this is the case, encourage the moss by keeping the surface clean of leaves and weeding out any grass or broadleaf plants. Delicately transplant clumps of the moss throughout the shaded area. Some enthusiasts prefer to mix up a fertilizer tonic of buttermilk or yogurt and water in a solution with at least eight parts buttermilk or yogurt to one part water and apply in the spring, spraying it over the surface. This is not strictly necessary—ordinary fertilizing with an acid-balanced fertilizer (such as aluminum sulfate) also suffices.

A stone pathway winds through a moss lawn.

How to Plant a Moss Garden

To start a moss garden from scratch, improve the soil by working in peat moss and organic compost to create the acidic soil moss prefers, a pH range of 4 to 7. Add slow-release fertilizer pellets or fertilizer formulated for acid-loving plants according to manufacturer's directions. Depending upon the amount of moss available to you, set in moss plugs at 2-inch intervals throughout the intended area. Or, you can mix

moss in a blender with water, or as some recommend, diluted beer and water. Mix only briefly, then further dilute the mixture in a bucket and pour the moss solution over the planting area. Cover with a thin coating of compost, and water thoroughly.

Do not overfertilize moss lawns, for they burn easily from too much nitrogen. An annual light application of an acid-balanced fertilizer at the appropriate season for your area will suffice; be sure to water the fertilizer in well.

If you prefer, there are substitutes for moss which are low growing and look similar. The prostrate thymes make a low-growing mat with tiny leaves, but they can't take extensive walking and they want at least some filtered sun or bright shade to do their best. Both baby tears and Irish moss tolerate shade and appear similar to a mossy covering but are hardy only to 0°F.

In continually moist situations, Irish moss makes an effective groundcover in the shade.

Moss doesn't have to be grown exclusively on the ground.

THE ALL-GREEN GARDEN

An all-green garden showing the many different shades of green possible.

So used are we to bursts of color—to being bashed with explosions of pinks, purples, yellows and reds in the flower garden—that it's easy to forget the subtle pleasures of an all-green garden. Every garden seems to yearn for a border to celebrate the esteemed Ms. Gertrude Jekyll, the late-Victorian garden designer who steered European gardens away from the formality of the ornamental garden to the relaxed attitude of the English cottage garden with its borders aflame with flowering plants from May to October. But there is another rewarding type of garden.

The Color of Green

Many monastic gardens are all green, and with reason. The faddish trend of color therapy has a basis in an ancient tradition that surrounding oneself with particular colors heals body and spirit. It does work, as painters in hospitals and schools can testify how color choice affects attitude and activity. After all, there is a reason waiting rooms in television stations are painted green and called greenrooms—the forest-colored walls are soothing to anxious stars waiting their turn next to be on stage.

That is not to say that any garden must be without other colors. But conceive of a garden room, be it ever so tiny, only planted in tones of greens. You don't need to deny yourself brightly colored flower displays in other areas, but enjoy one all-green area to slip into as the hot summer day just begins to edge into dusk. A small space surrounded with green hedges or shrubs and a comfortable bench becomes a peaceful place to sit for an afternoon cup of tea with a magazine, a report or to make notes for the next day's meetings.

The green garden can also be a seasonal interlude, a pause between flowering shrubs. A green garden using rhododendrons as the backdrop erupts with spring bloom and subsides to cool green during the heat of summer. If the rhododendrons are underneath deciduous canopy trees, then in the fall the green garden becomes enflamed with brilliant leaf color. Playing up this drama by all-green underplantings makes a dramatic statement in the garden. One Japanese maple dropping its bold golden-red leaves in a sea of green takes your breath away.

A Palette of Greens

Green may be restful, but it need not be boring. After all, green is not monochromatic. The layering of different greens within your green garden paints a complexity of color as eye-soaking as any row of neon-colored zinnias. Vegetation in

Ferns and hostas are the mainstay of an all-green fern garden, particularly in woodland gardens.

The all-green garden imitates nature.

Use variegated plants as focal points in an all-green garden. Splashes of white draw the eye, creating movement in the garden's design. Light-green plants appear to light up an especially dark part of the garden.

tones of lime, chartreuse, olive, grass green, pea green, forest green, kelly green, cobalt green, jade green, emerald, sea green, aquamarine or blue-green can be mixed and matched. And there are flowers in green, roses with a

A spray of white blooms brings seasonal color to the all-white garden.

greenish white hue, euphorbias with green flowers, trilliums and many others if you wish to introduce green flowers to the color scheme.

Certain color principles remain the same, whether you're working with shades of the same color or with completely different colors. Light shades stand out while dark shades recede. At the end of your all-green garden, a lime green feverfew (*Chrysanthemum parthenium* 'Aureum') against a dark holly will provide a color blast and make that part of the garden seem closer to you. Manipulating the space of your garden this way, just as a painter applies color to a canvas to add dimension, increases sophistication and appreciation of your own garden.

You can use any design for an all-green garden. A formal garden with clipped hedges has more maintenance, but its strict geometry has been beloved

This all-green tropical garden uses leaves to create textures. The cut-leaf pattern of the thin palm fronds is echoed in the fern leaves.

since the earliest gardens eons ago. Boxwood grows well in shade, as do a number of conifers, such as yew. In a small space you can create a formal garden room with clipped hedges, a bench or gravel paths edging borders. In a larger space, a wilder garden with untrimmed hedges backed against taller canopy trees can give you the sense of being in a secret grove even though you may be only steps from your own back door.

A woodland planting in all-green uses gray-leafed plants as accents.

Grouping plants with different leaf textures and colors makes a stronger display than intermingling them.

SUBTROPICAL AND TROPICAL GARDENS

Subtropical and tropical plants bring tropical romance and exuberance to a garden with huge-leafed, exotically colored plants that seem to conjure up the sweetly fragrant warm air and the gentle living of a far-away place. Most gardeners are under the impression, however, that one's climate limits most of the opportunities of living with unusual tropical plants. Not so! A bold experiment with tropical plants is open to all gardeners, regardless of where they live. The corner of any shady garden with a seating area, a patio or even a shady veranda can take on the air of the Amazon.

Tropical Plants in Cold-Winter Gardens

Gardeners living in a mild-winter climate can plant most of these tender plants outside and never worry about the frost's angry bite, but even gardeners in harsh winter areas can plant a tropical garden using pots that can be moved to overwinter in a protected location. You can transport a patio area or a narrow side yard to the tropics by adding six or seven large pots filled with the exotic look of tropical plants and their generously large blooms. Many bulbs with huge blossoms and strap-shaped leaves add to the tropical garden with their bold look even though they are perfectly hardy. You can dig up those that are not hardy every year and overwinter them inside.

When planted underneath a sheltering pergola or overhang, tender shade plants receive some frost protection from the structure in areas with light or unpredictable frosts. Similarly, next to the warmth of a house, tropical plants stay warmer overnight than out in the open. Use these situations to your advantage by planting

Crotons, usually known as a houseplant, can be summered outside in a container as a mainstay of your potted tropical garden. The splashy, colored leaves coordinate well with coleus's Persian carpet colors.

A tropical garden planting bed with coleus, salvia, shrimp plant and bougainvillea. You can duplicate this handsome planting on a patio or veranda, with plants set in containers.

The large, brightly colored leaves of the large-leaved caladium spring from a tuber that is easily started in the early spring. Grow it in pots or in the ground; but in cold-winter areas, dig up the tubers and overwinter them in a protected place.

tropical plants in these protected micro-climate situations even in relatively mild-winter climates.

Designing a Tropical Garden

When planning a tropical garden, throw out your inhibitions and think jungle. Mass together plants and break out all the color. Many tropical plants have dramatically large leaves. One example is the elephant ear plant; a description of the size of the leaf is poetic, if not quite accurate. Still, any plant with leaves that grow 3 feet long has a tropical feel. Caladiums, with their variegated colors, add light to the tropical garden. If there is some sun, try the bronzy red-leaved cannas, with their bright orange flowers.

Variegated plants such as spotted laurel (*Aucuba japonica* cultivars) look splashy next to taro root, which can also be grown in the water garden. Philodendrons, often house-plants, can come out to summer in this exotic atmosphere, and return safely indoors as temperatures fall at the end of summer.

There is no harm in adding hardy shade plants that match the tropical look of the exotics. Agapanthus (some varieties are hardy to 10°F) with its strap-like leaves fits right in a

tropical garden. Large-leafed hostas work extremely well incorporated into a tropical theme, although you might want to emphasize variegated leaf types for more explosions of jungle color. Tall ferns add a vertical lift to the tropical garden, and a potted tree fern that can overwinter indoors is a good addition, as well.

Evoking the Senses with Tropicals

Vines swirling up a structure and hanging down contribute to the look of a jungle. Fragrant plants also add to the tropical garden's mystique. Plant several honeysuckles together to present a tangled mass of bloom and green. Look for some of the tall grasses or grass-like plants with wide, spear-shaped leaves such as arundo, yuccas or even big-leaved canna. If they are not hardy in your area, grow them in pots or in the ground and overwinter in an unheated garage or basement.

Don't be shy about your tropical garden. Amass the most

The bright colors of the easily grown coleus sing out "tropical." Grow it as a perennial in warm-winter areas or as a tender annual in cold. Take cuttings in the fall, root in water and transplant into flats in a protected location over the winter. Set the cuttings out again in the spring after the last chance of frost.

curious, the most fragrant and the most colorful plants—all on a large scale—and have fun in the "tropics" right in your own backyard.

This dining pavilion with its corrugated roof looks over a tropical border.

HERBS AND OTHER EDIBLES

Intermingling herbs, lettuces and other tender greens into your flower beds and shady borders creates an edible landscape that pleases the eye as well as the palate. When space in a small garden is tight, and the gardener wants to also fill the larder, interplanting with edibles becomes both decorative and delicious. Consider tucking bright lime-green lettuces among the deep blue blossoms of lobelia, or use the bronzy-red leaves of lettuce (such as the heirloom variety known as 'Red Sails') to offset the deep forest-green colors of creeping ajuga. All the mints grow wildly in the shade to produce luxuriant groundcover, although you may want to check their invasive habits by isolating them in a raised bed or in a container sunk into the ground. Red-stalked chard sings out in a shady spot, providing both a color splash and nutritious greens even during the nippy seasons of the year.

Short-Season Crops
For the greatest success, choose plants with a short growing season for your shade garden. Often these plants are called "early" varieties. Look at the number of days to harvest—usually mentioned in seed catalogs or on the back of seed packages—or ask about seedlings if they are not marked in the nursery. These

Lettuce needs some shade during the hot summer months. Keep your salad bowl ingredients cool and moist and growing quickly. Look for types tolerant of heat to increase your success when temperatures soar into the 90s.

types mature quicker, making them more productive in the shade garden.

Matching Light Levels to Plant Requirements

When planting edible plants, matching plant to light level becomes critical because many of the plants producing edible pods, seeds, leaves or fruit require higher levels of light. You may have to disregard the prohibitions of garden manuals and do some experimentation specific to your own garden site.

Remember that most recommendations relate to commercial gardens with the need for high levels of productivity. In a home garden, a bucket of fresh fruit may be all your kitchen can use. In other words, a tree or plot that produces enough for a family is satisfactory, and the pleasure of picking your own fruit and vegetables outweighs concerns about measuring maximum output.

The easiest plants to grow in the shade are the lettuces and salad greens, as their tender leaves wilt and scorch out in full sun on the hottest summer days. A container or small cultivated *potager*, the French term for a small kitchen garden, in filtered

A small collection of potted lettuces, herbs and onions can keep the kitchen in salad for months. Start new pots monthly for a continual supply. To harvest, pinch off the outer leaves so the plant continues to produce. You can also move this portable collection to adjust for more or less sun.

Yes, vegetables and herbs too add an ornamental element to the shade garden.

shade suits their needs just fine. Lettuces, arugula, spinach and mesclun mixes—a variety of different delicious salad or stir-fry greens in the same package—produce a bowl of salad greens in about a month. Harvest the leaves just above the ground level when they are about 2 inches long, using scissors, and leaving the stems and leaves intact. The plants grow back quickly for two or even three more harvests.

Fruit from the Garden

Fruit trees earn their place in any garden with a changing display from season to season. Spring blooms lead to summer harvest. A tree hung with fruit is a beautiful object and a

reminder of the generosity of Mother Nature. In fall, the leaves tumble off in blazing colors. Most fruit trees require at least 4 hours of sun a day, so sun during the morning or part of an afternoon provides enough light to produce a crop. You must, however, work with a local cooperative extension agent or your favorite nursery to pick out the trees that suit your climate. Most fruit trees need a period of winter cold in order to bear, but there are many different varieties and there will be one to match your climate.

Carefully estimate the space available for a mature tree and choose either a dwarf (4 to 8 feet), mid-size (10 to 15 feet) or full-size tree (20 to 30 feet).

You can grow tomato plants in light shade—but expect lighter yields.

Consider the ornamental aspect of your edibles when planning the garden.

Blueberries are one of the most successful fruiting shrubs for the shade garden. Blueberries prefer partial shade, acid growing conditions and consistent moisture. Highbush blueberries can grow to a hedge, reaching up to 6 feet tall. Besides the harvest of the fruit, the shrubs are handsome in themselves, with leaves that turn colors in fall.

Herbs

Although planting instructions in many articles and books decree that herbs must have full sun, many herbs are careless about their growing conditions. As already mentioned, most of the mint family prospers in shade. Coriander needs moist soil and cool conditions to thrive—elements shade provides. Try an herb in a partially shady spot and watch how it prospers. Experiment with different shade locations from year to year. Parsley, thyme, borage, savory, fennel, oregano and lemon balm are among the many common herbs that do well in a shade garden. In other words, do not hesitate to plant herbs in your shade garden. Just monitor their growth and move them around to other sites in the garden if necessary.

Sun Lovers in the Shade

Don't be shy about planting beans, corn, tomatoes and cucumbers in a shade garden. Although direct sun increases production and sweetens fruits and vegetables, ground and air temperature play a part in the ripening process, as well.

If possible, plant only those varieties that ripen the earliest, sometimes called "early season" vegetables. Try to locate an area with at least two hours of direct sun a day. Keep a garden journal on varieties that produce the best for you. Edible plants grow well in containers, and if you have an old wheelbarrow that's not in use, it makes a great portable garden for lettuces or any short-rooted crops like radishes or globe carrots. With a wheelbarrow, you can chase the sun to increase the amount the plants receive.

Depending upon what your local nursery or garden center stocks, you may or may not be able to locate a good selection of early season varieties (check "Sources," page 164). Starting your own seeds may enable you to grow varieties that do best in the shaded edible garden. Remember, baby vegetables are the sweetest and tastiest, so harvest your plants early. Plus, keeping the plants harvested spurs additional flowering and growth.

Most mints do quite well in shade.

THE DRY SHADE GARDEN

The many kinds of cactus, with their incredible blooms and easy care, are great additions to any garden.

Gardeners in locations such as the arid Southwest, or California with its Mediterranean climate, do not have the luxury of water supplied from regular summer rains. Yet this is not as great a handicap as it might first seem. Many plants native to these climates have been hybridized and many plants have been imported to America from other scarce water areas around the world. In particular, the rich flora of the Mediterranean region, Australia and South Africa grace our dry gardens successfully. Bulbs, suc-culents, grasses, perennials, shrubs, vines and trees that don't mind drought or shade create a splendid garden with a wide variety of leaf texture, spring and summer bloom and gorgeous fall color.

Designing a Dry Shade Garden

A dry shade garden can be designed in any of the major styles, from woodland to Japanese. In fact, a Japanese-style garden can be one of the most water-saving designs. However, with canopy trees, a natural gar-den or a formal garden using appropriate drought-tolerant plants will be equally successful.

Choose plants for the dry shade garden with care. Not only must the plants accept a shady location, but they must adapt to dry conditions for part of the year. Many of them are not hardy, for they store water in their leaves. These succulents, with their fat juicy leaves, sur-vive by storing up water when it is plentiful and then like a camel draw it out when water is unavailable from the soil. This makes them vulnerable to freezing because as the temperature drops the water expands and ruptures the plant's cells. So before you set them out in your garden, make sure the plants are suited to your climate's temperatures.

The search for plants that tolerate both shade and drought is further complicated by the need to carefully match plants to preferred soil. Many drought-tolerant plants want a quick-draining soil when all the gardener can provide is a heavy clay amended with organic matter. Contact your county extension agency to get information about performing a soil test to accurately determine the quality of your soil. Amend the soil as necessary to bring it to its peak of both composition and nutrition. Select only those plants guaranteed to succeed in your garden's soil. After all, they will have to endure a long dry season during which they must sustain growth.

Selecting Plants

Many drought-tolerant plants have adapted by shrinking the size of their leaves to minimize the amount of water lost in transpiration. So when picking your plants, you may have to work to devise a list with a variety of leaf textures. There are oval-paddled cacti that withstand winter snow and wide-leafed groundcovers like ivy and native ginger that are drought tolerant. You can plant evergreen laurels and conifers that can successfully make it through hot dry summers, as well. Even some ferns such as the sword fern don't mind doing without water during the summer months, once they get established.

Grasses are particularly good choices for the dry shade garden, but with a few caveats. Some exotic grasses, such as pampas grass and some forms of miscanthus, have become exotic pests that escape from the garden and overrun native plants in the surrounding countryside. Others seed mischievously within the garden, adding to your weeding chores. However, there are a number, like carexes and fescues, that add color and form to the garden without any bad habits. Also consider plants with spear-like leaves, such as yucca, to complement grasses.

One of the joys of planning a dry shade garden is the palette of colors dry-loving plants come in. Many plants have fuzzy gray or blue-toned leaves, the better to deflect the suns rays and save water. Others come in light chartreuse greens. This lighter-toned palette can result in many successful combinations: Try

Sedums and cactus make good partners in part shade. Their different leaf structures create a rich and pleasing visual texture.

the gray of lamb's-ear with the dark green of rosemary; or mix blue-green grass with the gray leaves of snow-in-summer, accented with bits of purple-flowered alyssum.

Planting the Dry Shade Garden

Choose your time to set out new plants carefully, preferably just before the rains begin to provide the water that triggers their root growth. The better established they are as the fall rains end, the larger their root mass will be and the more effectively they can absorb available water from the soil during the dry seasons. If possible, water them weekly to carry them through the first dry season.

A mulch for the dry garden is essential. Use bark chips, compost or gravel, but spread it to a minimum of 3 inches deep. Make sure you water long enough to allow the water to penetrate through the mulch, or set irrigation lines underneath it. Regularly scrape back the mulch and dig into the soil for assurance that the soil is moist after watering, and watch that your plants look healthy, not wilted from too little water.

Dry shade plants want the soil to dry out in between waterings so check as the season progresses to make sure the timing of your watering suits their needs. Plants need more water after hot windy days, so if the weather changes, you may need to adjust your watering habits.

Containers in the dry shade garden need careful watching. Water them consistently, checking to make sure hot and windy conditions don't completely dry out the potting mix. Clustering containers behind a windbreak and mulching the tops with three or more inches of wood chips, rock or compost will help

Cactus don't always want to be in full sun. Many types prefer part shade. Spanish moss, cascading down from hanging pots, grows in part shade.

containers retain moisture. Terra-cotta pots are very porous: In hot weather any water in the soil mix wicks out through the pores of the terra-cotta and evaporates, so the mix dries out quickly. Choose pottery with a heavy ceramic glaze; this helps to maintain water in the potting mix.

But you can also seal terra-cotta pots with a masonry tile seal (available at hardware stores). Clean off both inside and outside surfaces of the terra-cotta pot. Brush on a coat of the seal, which looks like milky paint but dries clear with a matte finish. If desired, paint the outside of your pots with latex paint to add color after the seal has thoroughly dried.

It surprises many gardeners that pelargoniums grow in the shade. Here, established geraniums succeed in the dry shade garden with a snake plant.

A SHADE GARDEN OF CONTAINERS

Gardeners have long taken plants from the wild to bring back and grow within the confines of a container. Terracotta pots were invented eons ago, and filled up with flowers and plants in the rooftop gardens of the Babylonians or the stairways of middle-class apartment dwellers in Caesar's time. Today, many people live in apartments without a plot of land to tend, but well-planted containers can overflow on balconies, windowsills or rooftop ledges.

Containers solve many garden problems. They provide a safe habitat for plants susceptible to nibbling by wild creatures—from deer to gophers. They are portable for the protection of tender plants in a harsh climate. And they fill groundless spaces with living color and leafy texture.

Potted Plants for Every Use

Many a patio comes alive with a collection of pots planted up with bulbs, annuals, perennials or trees. With a collection of container-grown plants, you can reach out the kitchen door for any number of herbs that are just an arm's length away. A planter of bamboo provides a curtain of privacy between neighboring porches. You can move a fragrant plant, such as daphne, next to a favorite bench to enjoy its delightful perfume during bloom; then move it back to the best growing site for the rest of the season. When a tender plant is grown in a pot, there's no worry about freezing for you can easily whisk it into a protected location when frost starts to sparkle on the rooftops.

A colorful bank of pots overflowing with impatiens enhances an entryway or narrow side garden.

Depending upon the size of your pot, you can grow anything from the tiniest daffodil, with a bloom not more than a half inch wide, to a full-grown Japanese maple, spreading out its branches to provide enough shade for a full patio table.

Remember that a square pot or container holds more potting mix than a round-sided one. Match the size of the pot to the plant, and when you transplant to a larger pot, give fast-growing plants much bigger pots. Be sure that plants don't outgrow their pots, for potbound plants—whether 4-inch starter plants or large trees—become stunted if their roots don't have enough room.

Light Requirements for Potted Plants

Try growing almost anything you like in a pot, watching its growth pattern to tip you off to the suitability of the site you

A potted salad garden produces tomatoes, cucumbers and lettuce on this partly shaded rock wall.

have chosen for it. As the light changes with the seasons, the plant may become long and leggy, a sure sign it needs more light. If so, simply move it to a brighter spot. If a potted plant accustomed to bright light comes into bloom, move it next to a shaded bench or under a veranda for special display without doing it harm and actually extending the time it remains in flower. After the bloom has finished, move it back to its normal spot.

Working with a cluster of containers sharpens a gardener's aesthetic sense. Experiment in matching the shape of the container with the shape of the plant. A tall slender container looks dynamic with an upward burst of an ornamental grass. A bright blue-and-white porcelain container matches the sapphire blue of lobelia pouring over the top and down its sides. A collection of pots, all in the same colors and planted with identical plants, makes a bold statement marching up to a front door or entry stairs. Pots, in shades from forest green to celadon and planted with variegated hydrangeas, will enliven the corner of any shaded deck.

Creative Containers

By all means, have fun with your containers—rearrange them by the seasons, by bloom color or by whim. Creative gardeners paint large pots to match

Pots of bonsai give a Japanese garden flavor to a brick patio. Consistent watering is essential to maintain bonsai pots. Seedlings from Japanese maples often spring up underneath mature trees. Transplanting and training young trees into bonsai subjects can become an absorbing specialty for the gardener.

house colors, others use pots in place of architectural columns, boldly marching down a border or walkway. Old shoes, cracked teapots or colorful imported oil tins can add a touch of whimsy to your collections with their one-of-a-kind look.

One useful container plant contented to grow in shade is boxwood, which can be shaped into topiaries. Most appropriate to formal gardens, boxwood sheared as a topiary can accent borders, point the way to a bench, sit on top of a column or flank an entry stairway.

Container Care

To be successful with containers, you must remember that the plants they hold are your captives, restrained by the walls of their pot. Careful attention to regular watering and feeding of containers is essential for success, because their roots can draw only nutrients and water from their potting mix. Use a good quality potting mix for

Plants as dissimilar as ferns and impatiens grow together successfully in pots.

your containers, preferably one you purchase. (Plain garden soil often becomes a concrete-like block in the container.) Adding a time-release pelleted fertilizer regularly provides the nutrition essential for healthy growth. Read and follow label directions so that you don't over- or under-feed your plants.

Do not cluster containers too closely, for all plants need good air circulation to prevent disease. If possible, connect the containers to a drip irrigation system so they will be watered regularly.

Adding a pot to the broken seat of an old chair makes a whimsical container.

THE ALL-WHITE GARDEN

One of the most famous of all-white gardens, Sissinghurst is now open to the public.

One of the most famous all-white gardens is that of Vita Sackville-West, at Sissinghurst Castle in England. All-white describes a garden with plants that only bloom in white, although Vita did include some of the palest icy-pink blooms. Wandering through an all-white garden, a visitor is struck by the refreshing quality of the crisp green of the leaves and how they set off the fresh sparkling white of the blooms.

An all-white garden is even more outstanding as a shade garden. White in the shade seems to dance and shimmer, standing out more intensely than white in the sun. It is said that Vita Sackville-West got the idea for her all-white garden from seeing the white blossoms in the dusk, as she traveled through her garden to the dining room. This green and white formula is not as strict as it might seem once you include the host of variegated green plants with their striped, speckled or spotted leaves that look like the sun is lighting them from behind.

The Colors of an All-White Garden

Variegated plants usually have stripes of white and green, although some, such as lung-wort, can be mottled or spotted. Once you begin to experiment with slipping them into your

This mix of white-flowered plants uses large-leaved caladium as a dramatic backdrop to salvias, white-flowered cleome and pots of bedding begonias.

Gray-leafed plants work well in the all-white garden.

landscape scheme, you may find yourself devoted to variegated specimens. You can become a compulsive collector of variegated plants, for the leaves of bulbs (from tulips to iris), grasses, shrubs and small trees all come in some version of variegation. It is easy to choose low-growing plants, mid-sized shrubs and perennials and taller shrubs and even trees to fill out any garden plan.

You can also design swathes of different colors throughout your all-white garden, and increase your palette by including greens of different shades. The bright lime green of golden feverfew will perk up the darkest shady corner as if a floodlight were trained upon the spot. Hostas present a whole range of colors in themselves, from a light, bright, freshly minted green down to a deep, almost sea-blue green ... as well as a whole host of variegated shades.

An all-white shade garden is the perfect place to grow one of the hardiest roses, 'Iceberg', a floribunda rose. Floribundas are the result of a cross between polyantha roses and hybrid teas so they are a relatively new kind of rose. 'Iceberg', hybridized in 1958, maintains a fine reputation for its flowers, borne in clusters of a clean white color. The leaves are as virtuous in their dark green as the flowers in white; overall, the plant shows a remarkable resistance to rust and other fungal infections. 'Iceberg' needs a couple of hours of direct

sun, but will tolerate some filtered shade for the rest of the day. There is a climbing version of 'Iceberg' that is very vigorous, scrambling up over fences or along a pergola or trellis. The shrub form also grows quite large (up to 6 feet tall) but takes to pruning lower if you wish to contain it. 'Iceberg' looks particularly effective in front of a long dark hedge, the white flowers popping out from the dark background.

Another invaluable plant for the all-white garden is the little annual white groundcover alyssum, which really tolerates shade. White-blooming hydrangeas, snowball-blossomed viburnum and of course the old favorite white flowering

pelargonium pick up the theme throughout the summer. Half barrels packed with white pelargoniums or impatiens can accent an entryway or edge a patio.

When you are choosing plants for the shade garden, remember that white draws the eye forward: to foreshorten your garden, then, place a white plant, or a variegated green-and-white one, at the back of the planting. If you want to lengthen the appearance of your garden, start with the light green shades at the front of the planting and accentuate the distance by gradually slipping in darker and darker foliage toward the back of the planting area.

The blooms of white cleome, dahlias, white cosmos and bedding begonias glow in the twilight.

THE SHADY BOG GARDEN

A natural low spot in a shady woodland garden is easy to convert into a tiny pond, complete with shade-loving bog plants.

Searching out these plants has become increasingly easy because many gardeners have discovered the joys of plants that prefer wet feet ... resulting in sections of nurseries, as well as some mail-order catalogs, devoted to these types of plants.

If you don't have a spot in your garden that stays wet all year long, it is not hard to create one. One caveat: Once you have planted it, you will have to maintain its wet conditions.

Creating a Bog

To create a bog, scrape out a depression about 18 to 24 inches deep in a roundish shape that is not too regular—the bog should look natural—and as large as you want. Remove any sharp rocks, smooth the bottom and slope the sides to a 45-degree angle. Use old rug or fiberglass wall insulation to line the bottom. Cover the depression with a PVC plastic pool liner, making sure to seat the liner firmly on the bottom. Smooth out the liner and fasten it at the edge of the depression with large rocks. Depending upon the size and shape of the pool, you will have to make small tucks at the top edge of the liner as evenly around the top as you can. There is no need to cement the rocks in place, but arrange them so the liner is held securely and the edge is hidden by the rocks.

Making the Filler

In a wheelbarrow or large container, mix up the bog muck by adding two parts of sand to one part peat moss or oak leaves, and then stir in one part commercial potting mix. Add water, stir and let the mixture sit at

The bane of many gardeners is a shady spot with soil that remains soggy all year 'round. Ordinary garden plants want their roots to breathe, and many plants simply don't tolerate wet feet. To the despair of the gardener, these more finicky types may turn up their toes, and the gardener finds the compost pile accumulating the remains of unsuccessful plantings. Like the

old saying of turning lemons into lemonade, an adventurous gardener can use the boggy conditions to their advantage with plants that prefer soggy living areas.

Of course, when one thinks of all the marshes and cool wet areas bordering lakes and streams, it makes perfect sense that there are myriad plants that prefer mucky conditions.

least 24 hours to absorb the water thoroughly. Then shovel it into the bog area. During hot spells, you may have to add water if the bog begins to dry out. Remember—these plants are not water plants: They don't want to be floating in water, they just want swampy soil. Set in the plants as you would normally, taking care not to use sharp tools that might puncture the liner.

Choosing the Plants

Once the work of creating the bog is done, you can get down to choosing the plants. First look at the shape of the bog, and whether or not it is to be viewed from all sides. Like a flower arrangement, the order of the plants needs to be unified; and the smaller the bog, the fewer types of plants should be used. If it is to be viewed from all sides, then the front, sides and back need to have equally charming outlooks. Before setting plants in, practice a bit by laying out your plants in their containers to come up with an arrangement that pleases you.

Start in the middle of the bog and plant your tallest plants there. As you work forward to the edges, the plants become

smaller. But you don't want this to look too formal, so break the line here and there as you progress, suddenly inserting a taller plant in front of a smaller plant.

If the bog is viewed only from one side, then plant it as you would a border, starting with taller plants at the back and creating levels of lower plants as you work to the front. Don't make the levels too regular, but interrupt the lines with variegated plants and smaller plants in the back of taller ones occasionally.

The edges of the bog are important, for plants there are planted in soil and must bridge the transition from garden to bog. Ajuga with bronze or variegated leaves adds color as it creeps along; planted close to the edge, it will creep over slightly. Bergenia, with big bold leaves, is another good choice, although it wants a bit of sun. Grasses can repeat the look of bog iris, unifying the bog garden to the surroundings. Although an annual, lobelia planted just after the bog is completed will spread quickly, filling in until the perennials take over.

Bog plants growing around the edge of a pond.

A Simple Bog Garden

You can also create a bog shade garden in a large container with no hole. Place the container on your patio or sink it in the ground. Plant a large glazed pot into the ground with the edge just showing 3 to 4 inches, then place plants inside and around the edge. Choose leaf color of variegated plants to harmonize with the planter. Although one large-leafed plant such as an elephant ear may make a bold statement, generally plants scaled to the size of the pot look more appropriate.

An island in the middle of the pond is an effective site to show off bog plants.

Forget-me-not self-seeds along a creekside, making it an effortless garden plant from year to year.

THE VARIEGATED SHADE GARDEN

Gardeners complaining that a shade garden seems boring without the bright flowers of the summer border—the petunias in radiant pink and purple shades or the zinnias with fiesta colors—have only to look at the variegated shade garden with plants blooming and leaf colors in much the same brilliance, to realize their error.

The leaves of variegated shade plants come not only in greens and whites, but also with the silver spots of the lungwort, the Persian carpet tones of coleus, the deep burgundy colors of carpet bugle and the cotton candy pink color of winter-creeper 'Emerald Gaiety' in the winter. Even ivy, which a gardener might think of as coming only in a uniform dark green, actually comes in bright limy shades, and rip-roaring yellow edged in green. But just naming these few varieties—what about caladiums and hostas—does an injustice to the vast colorful world of the variegated garden.

Letting Plant Color Define Space

The variegated shade garden reminds us, as gardeners, that we are painters of space and that the plants we set into our garden are as much an aesthetic choice as any artist who lays the first daub of color onto a bare white canvas. As garden artists, we are taking space and pouring in color. Green, with its soothing, calming effect, pleases us and seems a neutral backdrop—an undercoat in painting parlance—to the color touches that accent and highlight the rest of our garden borders. One of the wonderfully complicating factors—which is why gardening is anything but boring—is that the palette changes continuously with the seasons, and our living "painting" subtly changes as one day flows into another.

Choosing variegated leaves lets the shade border shimmer

Just a sample of the stunning leaf patterns a variegated garden offers.

with color. Remember the design principle that bright, light colors seem closer than the dark colors. Assess your planting space critically. If there seems to be a dark hole at the end of the garden, then planting variegated plants will set it alive with color and light, accenting and highlighting the area. If you want to make a small space seem bigger, choose plants with dark colored leaves, in tones of deep purples, burgundy or bronze such as the dark-toned cultivars of coral bells. To make the space appear to be light and filled with color, use plants with leaves that are light golden-yellow or lime green.

The end of a walkway is the perfect spot for an explosion of color from variegated plants. You can lead up to this focal point with contrasting or coordinating colors in the border, or use all green to provide a dramatic buildup to the variegated plants at the end of the walk.

Even used singly, coleus makes an impressive display. When planted together, with a variety of colors and patterns, the Persian carpet effect is dazzling.

Trying Out Different Plants

Experiment with your plantings and enjoy the different effects you can make by alternating light colored plants with darker plants. Start by using low-cost annuals to fine-tune your sensibility of what you like and what seems successful to you. If you fall in love with a plant at a nursery—and who hasn't gone for one plant and come back with a carload?—don't be hasty to set it into its permanent location.

Try the plant, still in its container, in different spots to find just the right location in the garden for its mature size, its color and the texture of its leaves. Watch the light fall on it to make sure you can meet its requirements and look how the texture of its leaves works with those that will be its neighbors. See how the color works into your scheme. Finally, when you are sure you have found just the right place, plant it in its permanent location.

Pink plumes of astilbe add a splash of seasonal color to the variegated garden.

A NARROW SIDE GARDEN

Shade plantings create a lush greenness via groundcovers accented by pots, transforming this stairway into something special. The geraniums thrive in the shade, and the progression of their blooms leads up the stairway. Blue lobelia adds trailing swatches of color to the scheme.

City dwellers are familiar with the problem of a shady side garden on one side of their urban garden. If the narrow, shady plot leads to a door, the gardener tackles it with determination because the route must be traveled daily. More often situated out of the main traffic flow, this little garden space may linger weed-filled and sadly ignored. With a little effort and imagination, side gardens offer a great opportunity to create a private retreat or a charming pathway filled with the jewels of the shady garden.

Plotting the Light in the Garden

Depending upon how the house is sited on the lot, and its relationship to the neighbor's house, gardeners will have different sun angles to cope with from day to day and from season to season. A house oriented east to west usually has a narrow side yard with only exposure to north light. A north-south facing house will have garden areas exposed to bright morning light but deep shade in the afternoon. Searching out plants suited to the changing light levels may be particularly challenging. Don't worry if some plants indicate unhappiness with their situation by growing gawky limbs or barely growing at all. Gardening is not an exact science; every gardener seems to move plants like furniture, looking for the perfect spot where the plant will be happy and grow well.

Designing the Garden

First consider the overall design style of your garden. If the narrow side garden is isolated, you can design it separately from the total garden. If it is in clear view of the main garden, it should be consistent with the overall style of the garden.

A number of possibilities exist. Narrow side gardens lend themselves to an ambling stroll in a natural setting such as a woodland garden with small trees or tall shrubs pruned carefully to let in light. A simple woodland solution might be a combination of spring bulbs, ferns and a groundcover. On the other hand, a brick path edged with boxwood pruned

A narrow side garden—right by the deck off the kitchen—makes a convenient location to grow herbs. Just an easy step to collect savory herbs for any meal you're preparing.

The shade cast by a tall walls makes a garden here impractical. Yet the artful arrangement of rocks and gravel creates an intriguing space. Adapt this style to a narrow, north-facing side garden.

formally makes a neat and clean appearance. Flowering shrubs behind the low hedges make a seasonal display but stay tidy. Or create a Japanese garden with gravel surrounding stepping-stones, a trickling fountain and a bamboo fence. Both are low-maintenance gardens that are always a pleasure to behold.

Working with Narrow Spaces

The visual focus of the side garden—long and narrow—gives the gardener a chance to highlight a special object or plant. If the space is to be a quiet retreat, a bench or chair can provide a focus. If the site is a passage, then the gardener can plan a particularly intriguing pathway edged by plants that give the eye pleasure as one strolls through the space. Plants with blooms or colored leaves can accent parts of the journey. In the confined boundaries of a small and narrow garden, plants with fragrant flowers or scented leaves can make the passage through the space a sensual pleasure, for the leaves release

their perfume as someone brushes against them.

Annual flowers in large pots set within the borders walk the eye through the space and can be changed from season to season to provide color and interest. A pergola or archway can add much in interest to a side garden, for stepping into a garden off a busy street and then passing through an archway provides a pleasurable transition and a heightened sense of arrival. Planting the arbor with blooming vines provides additional privacy and beauty.

Designing a Path

A careful assessment of size and space is critical for designing and placing a path. Size the pathway in proportion to the width of the space. In most cases, the minimum width should be as wide as a wheelbarrow. A passageway that is too narrow and cramped is not a comfortable experience, causing the pedestrian to worry about stepping on plants or scratching up against unwieldy shrubs.

A major concern for the narrow side garden is for plants to stay within the bounds of their space. If a boundary line of greenery is needed, it is essential to choose plants that can define the space without overstepping its borders. Shrub hedges such as pittosporum or

Proof that a narrow bed with part shade can be as color-filled as any.

privet can be severely pruned to keep to their space. Bamboo (clump bamboo, not runner types) is well behaved in a limited area. An evergreen vine trained along a fence will also stay nicely horizontal. As any enthusiastic gardener knows, a plant which grows too large for its space must be trimmed back regularly to allow passage—a situation that is almost always detrimental to the plant's health, not to mention its appearance.

Improving Soil Composition

Attending to the quality of the soil is always critical, particularly if the side garden has been fallow for years or if an ill-defined pathway has compacted the soil into the planting beds. As with any shady garden, work in plenty of organic amendments such as compost, along with a time-release pelleted fertilizer. This is essential for the long-term health of the plants (see pages 150-153).

A lath house covers the area in a narrow side yard between two houses. Transformed with a brick path and plantings of rhododendrons, ferns and azaleas, the side yard has become a stylish entryway.

❦ CHAPTER 5 ❧

PLANTS FOR THE SHADE GARDEN

This plant encyclopedia lists some of the myriad choices of satisfactory shade plants available in nurseries, seed catalogs and specialty mail-order houses. These are the best-known shade plants, well behaved in the small garden and promising great rewards of bloom or foliage in any garden bed.

The zones listed for the following plants indicate a general temperature range. The aspect of your garden site, its microclimate and the individual sturdiness of the plant all affect its ability to thrive in your garden. Gardeners willing to experiment—and to suffer some losses—can add many additional plants to their shade gardens, even though some of the plants may not normally be recommended for a particular zone or climate. Using containers and moving less-hardy plants to overwinter in a protected area will add to the spectrum of plants that survive in your climate.

A

Besides having nice foliage, flowering maples also have showy flowers.

The flowers of flowering maples range from red to blue; some are bicolored.

Abies

Fir

These evergreen trees won't suit every garden, but they are an evergreen that takes shade. They also add a handsome conical, Christmas-tree shape to the scene. Some types will take pruning of the lower limbs, which creates light in the area underneath for planting. Many are slow growing; others grow larger than appropriate for a small garden.

Growing Guide

Shade 1 to 2. Check with your local nursery for varieties that do well in your area. Many firs are high-altitude trees and will not succeed at lower elevations. Make sure to match the mature size of the tree with the planting space. Firs tolerate light shade but also consider a location with morning or afternoon sun. Make sure to provide consistent water the first growing season.

Species, Varieties, Cultivars and Hybrids

A. balsamea 'Nana', a dwarf variety excellent for containers or in rock gardens. Zones 3 to 7.

A. concolor 'Candicans', white fir. 'Candicans' is the bluest in color. The mature tree can be 50 to 70 feet tall. Zones 4 to 7.

A. pinsapo, Spanish fir. A good choice for a warm, dry garden.

Slow growing to 50 feet. Zones 6 to 11.

A. veitchii, Veitch fir. The new cones emerge eggplant purple. Takes full shade. Zones 4 to 7.

Abutilon

Flowering maple, Chinese bellflower

Gardeners have finally discovered the abutilon; fan clubs have popped up, collecting all the new *Abutilon* varieties—and with good reason: Shade-loving abutilons are easy to grow and gratifying with their hanging bell-shaped blooms in a variety of colors. And at 10 feet tall, they are the perfect height for a small garden. They have 6-inch-wide, maple-like leaves. There are evergreen, semi-evergreen or deciduous abutilons from which to choose.

The spiny foliage and flower spikes of bear's breeches give the plant a coarse texture.

Growing Guide

Shade 1 to 3. These fast growing shrubs need pinching at the branch tips to force bushy growth instead of long and straggly branches. Some types are fully hardy, others half hardy, so check with your local nursery for varieties appropriate to your climate.

Species, Varieties, Cultivars and Hybrids

A. x *hybridum.* This is the most common variety. Although some types bloom from April to June, white and yellow forms bloom all summer long. Grows as tall as 8 to 10 feet and spreads as wide. Zones 8 to 10.

A. megapotamicum. Grows to 10 feet tall with red and yellow hanging, lantern-like blossoms. Long branches allow it to be used in a hanging container or espaliered on a shady fence. Zones 8 to 10.

A. pictum 'Thompsonii'. Variegated yellow and green leaves in a mottled pattern. Zones 9 to 10.

Acanthus

Bear's breeches

A candidate for large spaces, the large leaves of acanthus and its tall, delphinium-like, white bloom stalks are a boon in neglected parts of the shade

garden that you want to naturalize. But take note of the plant's bad habit of sprouting from just the smallest bit of root, making it difficult to move or eradicate.

Growing Guide

Shade 1 to 2. Acanthus goes dormant with lack of water, so if you want leaves through the summer, water consistently. Plant in containers or in a space where it can naturalize.

Species, Varieties, Cultivars and Hybrids

A. spinosus, spiny bear's breeches. Thistle-like leaves and tall—to 4 feet—flower spikes. Zones 6 to 9.

A. mollis, bear's breeches. Quickly spreading throughout the garden through underground roots. The handsome, dark, shiny-green leaves are large and tropical looking. Pinkish-white bloom spikes rise up to $1^1/2$ feet tall in late spring. Zones 7 to 10.

The flowers of bear's breeches also make interesting cut flowers.

Japanese maples are great small trees for partially shaded areas.

Acer

Maple

Maples don't just have to be trees; there are varieties that stay low. Although most can be trained as a tree, they naturally bush out like a shrub. Many of the tree types can outgrow a small garden. Most are deciduous, but some are evergreen. Many grow well in shade. Look for types with good autumn color, highly ornamental stems and bark or attractive leaves during the growing season. Most maples do not like heat, drought or lack of winter chill, but there are some drought-tolerant types. Size ranges from about 10 feet to 70-foot giants.

Growing Guide

Shade 1 to 2, according to type. Maples, especially the tree types, need water throughout the growing season, so water deeply during dry periods.

Species, Varieties, Cultivars and Hybrids

A. crataegifolium 'Veitchii'. A tree with variegated green and white leaves that turn deep pink and purple in autumn. Slow-growing to 30 feet. Zones 6 to 8.

A. palmatum, Japanese maple. A beautiful small tree or large shrub with delicately cut leaves. Good choice for a Japanese-style garden, grove or woodland area. Slow-growing to 20 feet. *A. p.* 'Butterfly' has variegated pink, cream and green leaves. *A. p.* 'Dissectum Atropurpureum' forms a mound of bronze-colored foliage that turns brilliant in autumn. Zones 5 to 8.

A. japonicum, fullmoon maple. This small tree grows to 20 or 30 feet, but can also be pruned to a small shrub. *A. j.* 'Atropurpureum' carries beautiful purple leaves. Zones 6 to 8.

Achimenes

Related to gloxinias and African violets, these shade-tolerating plants grow from rhizomes in either erect or trailing forms. Their flashy flowers come in shades of pink, red and purples. Achimenes make excellent container plants to bring color into the shade garden or lath house. Use the erect types in borders or as drifts in woodland gardens, but use them as annuals

Acer saccharum *(sugar maple).*

The small size of Japanese maples makes them good choices as container plants.

Achimenes, the monkey-faced pansy.

or lift the rhizomes before the temperatures drop in the fall. Let the trailing types droop over walls or the edges of raised beds.

Growing Guide

Shade 1 to 2. Plant the rhizomes in a light, quickly draining potting mix as you would tuberous begonias. Keep the mix moist, but make sure the roots do not stay soggy. In cold winter climates, let the plants dry out after flowering, lift the rhizomes and store with your other bulbs. Tender to 50°F. Zone 10.

Species, Varieties, Cultivars and Hybrids

A. antirrhina. An erect perennial with trumpet-shaped 1¹/₂-inch red to orange flowers.

A. 'Paul Arnold'. Erect with purple flowers.

A. 'Peach Blossom'. Trails with funnel-shaped peach-colored blossoms.

Aconitum
Wolfsbane, monkshood

With a bloom stalk similar to delphiniums, the shade-loving aconite sends up long flower stems. Different varieties bloom from spring to fall. Tall 2-to 5-feet-high plants, they do well at the back of borders. But they go completely dormant in the winter, so mark their site so you leave space for them to reappear in the spring. Note that all parts of the plant are poisonous.

Growing Guide

Shade 1 to 2. A tall plant (up to 5 feet), monkshood looks dramatic in groups under canopy trees in a natural garden. Or place in the back of a shady border. Plant in rich, moist soil—monkshood wants consistent moisture.

Species, Varieties, Cultivars and Hybrids

A. napellus, garden monkshood. Blue or light violet flowers appear in late summer, rising up on bloom spikes.

A. n. 'Album'. White flowers that make a handsome display

The rich blue of monkshood is a knock-out in the late summer garden.

in the shade border or edging a pond or bog. Zones 5 to 8.

TREES FOR THE SHADE GARDEN

Trees define a garden. They can frame a view or star as the focal point on center stage. Trees filter sunlight, making the garden comfortable during the hot days of summer and creating an ever-changing backdrop of shadow and light.

With their changing costumes, trees make the garden a lively theater, full of visual drama and beauty. Opening with spring blossoms, a tree's performance proceeds with a delicate tracery of leaves against the sky. Some restrained types wait to bloom until summer, just as small fruit starts to appear on spring-flowering varieties. In the fall, enjoy the crescendo of colors as leaves turn a hundred brilliant hues before being stripped away to reveal the finale of bare skeleton branches silhouetted against the winter's

sky. Even the most jaded would have to admit trees put on quite a performance.

Trees are long-term residents of the garden, so take the time to choose them carefully. It is a pity to be forced to remove a tree because an unobservant or impatient homeowner didn't anticipate that 20 years of growth would find the tree bursting out of its space, rubbing against the roof, overhanging a neighbor's garage or darkening the garden with its shade. Some trees get so big it's like the proverbial elephant in a living room—you can't help but notice them!

So before you lose your heart to a tree, check that your space, weather and exposure suit a potential candidate. Then bring it home, introduce it to your garden and let it perform its effortless magic.

Bishop's weed is a very vigorous groundcover for shady places.

Aegopodium
Variegated bishop's weed

A low-growing—up to 4 inches—variegated, leafy plant. This is a perfect groundcover when you don't care about flowers. Small light green, white-edged leaves form a carpet. The plant spreads quickly. The variegated leaves are perfect to lighten the ground under an evergreen tree.

Growing Guide

Shade 1 to 2. Set in plants 4 inches apart in rich, moist soil.

Agapanthus adds a tropical feel to your shade garden.

For the best appearance, mow at least two if not three times a year.

Species, Varieties, Cultivars and Hybrids

Aegopodium podagraria 'Variegatum', variegated bishop's weed. The leaves are edged white, making the plant seem to shimmer in the shade. Some plants are all green, and you

should pull these up to maintain the variegation. Zones 4 to 9.

Agapanthus
Lily of the Nile

Individual 3-foot blossom stalks rise up over large, straplike leaves to a height of 16 to 24 inches. The flowers form in umbels in shades of blue or white. For a smaller scale, use the dwarf variety that grows to 8 inches. Agapanthus is drought tolerant after it has become established, making it excellent in the dry shade garden. Lovely clumps in drifts provide unusual globes of color to punctuate a border. Excellent standing alone as a long aisle planting. The dwarf variety is attractive in the front of borders. Both large and small types make excellent pot plants.

Growing Guide

Shade 1 to 3. In cold areas agapanthus are grown as a tender annual; there is a new type developed in England called 'Headborne Hybrids' hardy to

Ajuga is a great groundcover for its spring flowers, as well as its summer and autumn foliage.

Ajuga forms a nice, thick carpet of color.

Zones 6 to 9, though. Plant in moist, well-drained soil to get started. Once established, plants take drought. Where necessary, provide winter protection.

Species, Varieties, Cultivars and Hybrids

A. 'Alice Glouchester', forms large clumps with large umbels of white flowers in summer. Leaves not as wide as some varieties. Zones 9 to 10.

A. 'Liliput' (or *A.* 'Peter Pan'), is the dwarf form with dark blue flowers. Zones 9 to 10.

A. 'Hardy Headborne', can be overwintered in the garden in Zones 6 to 9.

Agonis
Peppermint tree

An excellent evergreen tree with leaves that smell of peppermint when crushed. A good lawn tree or espalier, its thin long leaves have a willow-like appearance. It has white blooms in spring to summer, and grows quickly to about 25 feet. This is an excellent tree to provide quick shade to a small garden. One tree can provide color in spring with its bronzy new leaves, and small spring to sum-mer white flowers. The filmy leaves make open, filtered shade—a perfect habitat for a large variety of shade flowers.

Growing Guide

Shade 1 to 2. The peppermint tree is tender at 25°F but if it freezes, may sprout back from the roots. Locate the tree where it receives at least 4 to 5 hours of sun a day. Zones 9 to 11.

Species, Varieties, Cultivars and Hybrids

A. flexuosa, peppermint tree. Grows quickly to 25 feet with a weeping habit. The new leaves in the spring are a bronzy color followed by tiny white flowers. *A. f.* 'Variegata' has variegated foliage.

Ajuga
Bugle weed

A low-growing ground cover valued for its leaves in combinations of white, dark purple, green and pink, and dark green with bronze flushes. Flowers rise up as spikes in colors of white, blue or pink.

Growing Guide

Shade 1 to 3. Spreading in a mat from 6 to 12 inches tall, ajuga tolerates some sun but can take full shade for part of the day. Space plants 6 inches apart. Will stand some dryness but is not drought tolerant and wants rich humus, loamy soil and consistent moisture. For best appearance, trim off old bloom spikes. Zones 4 to 8.

Species, Varieties, Cultivars and Hybrids

A. reptans 'Multicolor', has variegated leaves in shades of green, white and pink. Makes a wide carpet, spreading quickly to make a handsome groundcover.

A. r. 'Atropurpurea', has deep bronzy-purple leaves with dark blue flowers. Makes a wonderful chocolaty puddle of color in the shade garden.

The deep blue flowers of ajuga complement the foliage beautifully.

Akebia quinata, *the five-leaf akebia.*

Akebia
Chocolate vine

There are two varieties of this unusual vine with dark purple flowers that look like cups. To some, the flowers give off the fragrance of chocolate; others say vanilla. The flowers are followed by an edible fruit which is described as looking like a small sausage. Try akebia on a trellis or arbor where their flowers and fruits can be clearly seen. In mild climates they may stay evergreen; where temperatures dip below freezing they are deciduous.

Growing Guide

Shade 1 to 2. Unfussy about sun or shade, plant these vines where they have good support. You will have to tie them as they grow. Although not as invasive as some vines, they can be pushy. They benefit from radical pruning (as in down to the ground) yearly which will keep them under control.

Species, Varieties, Cultivars and Hybrids

A. quinata, five-leafed akebia. Five leaves in a whorl around the stem gives an airy appearance. Grows to 30 feet. Zones 5 to 9.

A. trifoliata, three-leafed akebia. Vine grows to 30 feet. Not as fast-growing as the five-leafed akebia. Zones 5 to 8.

Allium
Ornamental onion

Alliums (over 500 species strong) tolerate sun and produce finely cut flowers, many of which dry successfully. Some are fragrant, and few give off onion smell unless stems are crushed. They are resistant to insects, disease and deer. Depending upon variety, they may suit the dry shade garden. Small types (up to 6 inches) fit into rock gardens. Larger types makes splashy displays in borders with light shade. Both the leaves and the flowers are edible in some varieties such as chives or Chinese chives.

Growing Guide

Shade 1 and 2. Plant bulbs in clumps for a natural look. Plant the bulbs in the fall and provide moisture during the growing season. Divide when clumps become large and flowering diminishes.

Allium senescens *'Summer Beauty'.*

Allium giganteum.

Species, Varieties, Cultivars and Hybrids

A. cristophii, star-of-Persia. Large clusters of lavender to deep sapphire flowers bloom in June. Makes a fine dried flower. Plant grows to 15 inches. Zones 5 to 9.

A. giganteum, giant allium. Great balls of lavender flowers sway 4 to 5 feet tall. Zones 5 to 9.

Star-of-Persia.

A. moly. Good for dry shade gardens, this allium's yellow spring flowers brighten shady areas. Give morning sun, if possible. Zones 5 to 8.

A. sativum, garlic. Garlic makes a great border edge or in dots throughout. Both the leaves and the white powder-puff flowers are edible.

A. senescens, lavender globe lily. This lily forms clumps that grow larger every year. Great balls of lavender-pink blooms come out in summer. Zones 5 to 9.

A. triquetrum. The triangle-shaped stem is distinctive, as is the onion fragrance when crushed. The bell-like flowers, and stems, are edible. Will naturalize in great drifts. Can be invasive. Zones 7 to 9.

A. tuberosum, Chinese chives. Long, thin leaves droop to 12 inches. Flowers are small white

VINES

Vines are often described as the "walls" of the garden, for they have the ability to decorate vertical surfaces on their climb up to the light. They soften and clothe walls, fences and the sides of buildings as they go. You can use vines to throw a green covering over an unsightly outbuilding, to beautify a neighbor's scratchy fence or add a veneer of civilization over a pile of rubble.

Vines can be either deciduous or evergreen. So if you wish to use a vine to create privacy, consider an evergreen type for year-round effect. There is good variety within the category of vines, with everything from dainty vines running up a string in a container, to spreading types that grow to 30 feet long, rambling over everything in their path. You can choose a vine that will be covered with fragrant blossoms, or find one with leaves that turn red and purple in the fall.

globes which look decorative when separated and floated on soups or in salads. Chop leaves for garlicky chive flavor. Zones 7 to 9.

Allium moly.

Amaryllis belladona.

Amaryllis
Belladona lily, naked lady, surprise lily

These bulbs can be found throughout mild-winter areas. Many a naturalized stand of belladona lilies serves as silent testimony to deserted farms and homesteads, for even though totally neglected they continue to thrive. Although sun-loving, they are shade tolerant and will bloom in light shade. The leaves come up in the spring, then die back in early summer. A little later the flowering stems follow, producing trumpet-shaped fragrant flowers in pink or white; when used as cut flowers, they perfume a whole room. It makes a dramatic border plant, or can be an edging plant along driveways for greenery in the spring and spectacular bloom in summer. Don't plant over the bulbs when their leaves have died back. For a similar appearing plant that is more cold tolerant see *Lycoris squamigea*.

Growing Guide

Shade 1 to 2. Plant the bulbs just level with the soil. Break up clumps and move only just after blooming. Zones 6 to 10.

Species, Varieties, Cultivars and Hybrids

A. belladona 'Hathor', is a white version.

Ampelopsis
Porcelain berry

A deciduous, twining vine with leaves that look like ivy, porcelain berry is loved for its annual shiny blue berries that follow small green flowers. The berries will attract birds to your garden.

Growing Guide

Shade 1 to 2. The vine climbs by twining around, so if you have a smooth wall or fence, provide string or wire for it to climb. Prune just to guide it where you want it.

Species, Varieties, Cultivars and Hybrids

A. brevipedunculata 'Elegans'. 'Elegans' stays smaller than

'Honorine Jobert' is a good cultivar of the Japanese anenome.

other cultivars and has variegated leaves tinged with white and pink. Although there are other types of *Ampelopsis*, this one stays smallish and is well behaved even in hanging baskets. Zones 4 to 8.

Anemone
Windflower

Graceful plants that bloom in the shade—especially the Japanese anemone, which provides autumn blooms in pink or white. Plant these at the back of the shade border, for the blooms arch up. Use also as a spreading groundcover under tall canopy trees for a meadow of fall bloom.

Growing Guide

Shade 1, 2 or 3 depending on species. These perennials have tubers or fibrous roots, and under the right conditions spread, though they are not invasive. Provide even moisture and a rich humus soil. Some types bloom in the fall. Zones vary by species.

Species, Varieties, Cultivars and Hybrids

A. x *fulgens*, scarlet windflower. Large bright red flowers with black stamens mark this handsome shade plant. Grows to 1 foot tall. Zones 8 to 9.

A. x *hybrida*, Japanese anemone. Clumps of plants send up 3- to 4-foot-tall swaying

Anemones often come in delicate, pastel shades.

Windflowers.

Species, Varieties, Cultivars and Hybrids

A. canadensis, common columbine. A perennial forming clumps 12 inches wide and up to 2 feet tall. Blooms in early summer with a number of flowers on tall stems. Zones 3 to 9.

A. hybrids. Columbine hybrids grow up to 3 feet tall, although there are shorter—1 foot tall—varieties. The spurred flowers are large and come in a combination of pastel shades. Zones 4 to 9.

stalks capped with pink or white blooms in the fall. Should be mulched in cold winter areas. Looks graceful mixed with ferns underneath tall canopy trees. Zones 6 to 8.

A. nemorosa, wood anemone. Growing 1 foot tall, a white-flowered anemone that prefers shade. Makes a good ground-cover for a woodland garden. Zones 5 to 8.

Aquilegia
Columbine

Not a long-lived perennial, but one beloved in the shade garden for its fine, gray-green foliage and exquisite flowers that seem to hover above the plants from spring to summer. The large flowers with long spurs come in pastel shades and in some varieties with double petals. Hummingbirds love the flowers for their honey nectar. The plants, although they last only two to three years, reseed. Even the hybrids will reseed, although the new plants will not look like the parents.

Growing Guide

Put in plants or sow seeds in early spring or late fall. Use columbine underneath shrubs or in shady borders. Columbine grows well in containers.

Aquilegia 'McKana Giants'.

Aruncus
Goat's beard

A ferny-foliaged perennial that forms hummocks in moist soil. Goat's beard resembles astilbe, but the bloom stock with white flowers resembles tufts of white hair.

Growing Guide

Plant in humus-rich soil and water consistently. Cut off plumes as they dry up to keep the plant attractive.

Species, Varieties, Cultivars and Hybrids

A. aethusifolius. The arching flower stems reach 16 inches tall above divided foliage.

A. dioicus. A tall form, growing to 6 feet tall. Zones 4 to 8.

Asarum
Wild ginger

One of the finest of groundcovers for a shady garden, tolerating even the deepest shade. Depending upon the variety, can be drought tolerant. Wild ginger bears an inconspicuous, brownish flower, but the leaves are bright green and heart-shaped. There are native species tolerant of almost any climate.

The glossy foliage of European wild ginger makes it a popular choice for shady locations.

Growing Guide

Shade 1 to 3. Set out wild ginger into a rich, moist soil. Keep watered until it is established. Add fertilizer yearly. Check varieties for zones.

Species, Varieties, Cultivars and Hybrids

A. canadense. The most hardy variety, with kidney-shaped leaves 6 inches wide and dark brown flowers with a purple hue. Zones 3 to 6.

A. caudatum. A West Coast native plant, spreading a glossy green carpet underneath trees or tall branching shrubs. Leaves are heart-shaped and can be 4 to 7 inches wide. Zones 5 to 8.

A. europaeum. Dark, glossy kidney-shaped leaves spread to form a groundcover about 6 inches tall. Zones 5 to 8.

Astilbes are great plants to brighten up moist, shady spots.

Gingers, like Asarum caudatum, have showy but hidden flowers.

Astilbe

False spirea, meadow sweet

With feathery flower plumes in shades of white, pink, salmon and red, astilbe is queen of the shade gardens. Varieties bloom from May through August, so choose carefully to provide a long succession of flowers. The leaves are delicately cut and much like ferns; even out of bloom, they present an attractive appearance. Some types grow to just 12 inches high, while taller types stretch up to 36 inches when in bloom. The flowers make lacy cut blooms which dry well.

Growing Guide

Shade 1 to 3. Astilbe likes a continuously moist, rich humus soil. Cut back the blossoms after bloom and divide the clumps every 4 to 5 years. Zones 4 to 9.

Species, Varieties, Cultivars and Hybrids

A. chinensis 'Pumila'. A smaller (to 12 inches) variety good for the rock garden. Zones 5 to 8.

Athyrium

Ferns

Deciduous or semi-evergreen ferns. Can be hardy or tender depending upon variety. Takes a bit of effort to remove the dead fronds as they die back.

Growing Guide

Shade 1 to 3. Set these ferns into rich moist soil at the back of the planting border or

The fine-textured lady fern is a very hardy fern for gardeners in Northern areas.

scattered throughout a woodland garden. Trim off dead fronds for a neater appearance.

Species, Varieties, Cultivars and Hybrids

A. filix-femina, lady fern. A hardy fern that adapts well to the garden environment. Grows up to 3 feet tall but looks finely drawn. Zones 4 to 9.

A. nipponicum 'Pictum', Japanese painted fern. One of the most unusual ferns and a great addition to the variegated shade garden with its gray and burgundy splashes along the center ribs of the fronds. Deciduous. Grows 1 to 2 feet tall. Zones 4 to 9.

Azalea (See *Rhododendron*)

Astilbes have plumes in shades of pink, red, white or lavender.

B

Bamboo

Although bamboo technically is a grass (not a shrub) these plants are useful as shrubs in the garden, presenting unusual textures and a vertical thrust wherever needed. If you are planning a Japanese-style garden, you will definitely want to include bamboo. Look for dwarf bamboos, clump bamboos for a fountain-like explosion of foliage or running bamboos to make an effective hedge.

Growing Guide

Shade 1 to 2. Bamboo has two primary growing types, clump and running. The clump type expands gradually. But the roots of the running bamboo are exceedingly invasive, coming up beyond fences into neighbor's gardens. Choose a variety carefully with these traits in mind. Although many bamboos are tropical, some types are quite hardy. Heavy mulching helps protect roots in cold winter areas.

Species, Varieties, Cultivars and Hybrids

Pleioblastus chino gracilis, fountain bamboo. This small bamboo grows only to 3 to 4 feet with leaves striped in white. Zones 7 to 9.

Fargesia nitida syn. *Sinarundinaria nitida.* A bamboo that looks best growing in the shade. Frost hardy, this bamboo grows to 12 feet with culms that start out purplish and mature almost to black. Growing as a

The flashy flowers of tuberous begonias can be the shining stars of the shade garden.

clump bamboo, it is easily contained in patches in the garden and amenable to container culture. Zones 7 to 10.

Begonia
Begonia

Bedding begonias have proven themselves sturdy bloomers in shades of pink, red, white and salmon ... oftentimes with bronze leaves. When planted with ferns, they can look like small wildflowers. Tuberous begonias have larger flowers that glow in neon colors, brightening up any shady area. Each year the tubers of the tuberous types grow larger, so overwintering them will increase bloom from year to year. They are very tender, so allow them to dry out as fall approaches and store them with your other bulbs. Both kinds are great in hanging pots and patio containers.

Growing Guide

Shade 1 to 2 for bedding types; shade 1 to 3 for their tuberous cousins. Set bedding begonias in a well-worked bed and water generously, but watch the leaves for fungal disease. If disease occurs, water only in the morning and pinch off infected leaves.

Start tubers of the tuberous kinds indoors in flats in January or February. Nestle tubers in

Fibrous begonias are heat tolerant, and come in a variety of foliage and flower colors.

the potting mix about halfway up the sides of the tuber. Keep the mix moist until they begin to leaf out. Then transplant them into a planting bed or container. Grow in humus-rich soil and keep humidity up in hot, dry areas. Watch for fungal disease and snails.

Species, Varieties, Cultivars and Hybrids

B. x *semperflorens*, bedding begonia. Dwarf begonias grow 6 to 8 inches while taller strains grow to 12 inches. The leaves can be green, bronze or variegated.

B. x *tuberhybrida*, tuberous begonia. A summer-flowering tuber with pendulous and upright forms that flowers in shades of white, red, pink, orange and yellow.

The large flowers of tuberous begonias look beautiful floating in dishes of water.

PERENNIALS

Who doesn't sing the charms of perennials in our gardens? They bring colorful foliage and flower with reckless abandon. Every gardener loves them. Perennials grow, flower and produce seed for at least two years, often much longer. There are tender perennials that are killed by frost, and hardy perennials that survive frost but may go dormant. Plant perennials in late fall or early spring depending upon your climate. In cold weather areas, perennials need to establish themselves—developing healthy roots before the cold season begins. In mild winter areas with summer drought, perennials need to develop a large root mass to help cope with the diminished rain cycle.

The pretty red, white or pink flowers of bergenia first appear in the spring.

Bletilla
Wood orchid

An easy-to-grow small bulb with tiny 1-inch white or pink orchid blossoms that can be planted in the garden or in containers. Wants shade all summer long and prefers the culture of rhododendrons and azaleas. The miniature orchid blossoms in white or pink are good cut flowers.

Growing Guide

Shade 1 to 3. In the fall in mild winter areas or spring in cold winter areas, set the bulbs in the ground 2 inches deep and 6 inches apart in a lightly shaded area well worked with compost to drain easily and maintain slightly acid soil. Fertilize in the fall or spring. Keep the plant slightly moist during the growing season. Lift from gardens in severe winter areas and keep moist during dormancy.

Species, Varieties, Cultivars and Hybrids

B. striata, wood orchid. A single bulb produces long grass-like blades and a bloom stalk with 10 to 12 white or pink blooms. Zones 6 to 8.

Bergenia
Bergenia

Great large leaves in glossy green are topped with small clusters of pink flowers. Useful in the shade as a groundcover, bergenia makes a handsome display when used in a large area. Excellent as a foil for fine-leafed ferns or underneath rhododendrons and azealeas.

Growing Guide

Shade 1 to 3. Once established, bergenia can take drought, although it looks better with water. Watch out for snails and slugs. Divide when clumps begin to look messy.

Species, Varieties, Cultivars and Hybrids

B. cilata. Although slightly tender, this elegantly leafed type is less common. New leaves emerge with a bronzy tint. Flowers come in white, pink or purple. Zones 5 to 9.

B. crassifolia. Winter-blooming bergenia. This late winter blooming variety is the most common. Flower stems rise up above the leaves which may stand 20 inches high. Zones 4 to 9.

Bergenias have rosettes of thick leaves that often turn shades of red in winter.

Brassica
Flowering kale, flowering cabbage

Easy to start from seed (but readily available as transplants in six-packs), flowering kale is one of the more unusual annuals popular not for its flowers but for its variegated white-and-green or pink-and-green leaves. In mild winter climates, it will overwinter—continuing until it blooms with yellow, edible flowers in late spring. Use it in containers, as edging or as bright flowers in the shade border. It grows large, up to 24 inches, and is as showy as any annual in full flower. Both the leaves and the blossoms are edible. Stir-fry leaves when young, or use in salads. Toss the flowers on top of soup or in salads for dots of bright yellow.

Growing Guide

Shade 1 to 3. Sow the seeds in midsummer or set the transplants into a shady area by late summer for fall use; alternately plant in earliest spring for spring bloom. Plant and grow like any member of the cabbage family. If aphids attack, simply wash off with water. Repeat washings as necessary. Work in an organic time-release, pelleted fertilizer when you plant. Mulch with 4 to 6 inches of organic compost.

Species, Varieties, Cultivars and Hybrids

B. hybrids. Plants grow up to 14 inches high, so give them space to grow. You can harvest the edible leaves. When the plant finally blooms, the bright yellow flowers are also edible. Intermix the flowering kale with pansies for a colorful and edible garden edging.

Flowering kale produces a lot of bright color in late summer and autumn.

BULBS

Although many gardeners think of bulbs as growing only in full sun, there are varieties which prefer shade while others tolerate shade easily. Still, the crafty gardener who wants a fine spring display and has only an area of deciduous trees, can pack the ground underneath them with early spring-blooming bulbs. These bulbs burst out in blossom before the trees awake from their winter dormancy, effectively blocking the sun with their leafy canopy.

Shade-loving bulbs make an impressive display in the woodland garden. Some types naturalize year after year to create great drifts of color. Still others, set in containers, can provide seasonal accents to a small terrace garden or provide focal points along a border or at the turning of a pathway. Choose bulbs to bloom successively so that you have something bursting into bloom from early spring to late fall.

Generally, plant spring-blooming bulbs in the fall, summer-blooming in the spring and fall-blooming in July or August. The rule for planting depth is to set the bulbs in the ground about three times as deep as their height. If you cannot tell which side of the bulb is the top, plant bulbs on their side. Feed bulbs with an all-purpose, time-release fertilizer in early spring so that the bulbs will absorb the nutrition they need to create luxuriant blossoms the following year. After blooming do not cut off the leaves of any bulb until they begin to wither and turn yellow.

Several species of brassica are ornamental as well as edible.

Brassica

Giant red mustard

Red mustard is one of the easiest plants to grow, readily sprouting up from casually sown seed. Red mustard is edible *and* makes a long-lasting and handsome foliage plant in a flower border. Unfussy about the amount of shade it receives, it makes an unusual bedding plant with deep burgundy-red, creased leaves. In favorable conditions it will grow to 4 feet, throwing up a bloom stalk with edible flowers that can reach 5 feet tall. Use the young foliage as an edible green, cooking like spinach. Leaves are spicy hot when young, but become mild when mature. Slow to bolt, when it finally does, let some seed self-sow and use the edible flowers in salads or to top soups. You can even save the seeds to make your

own mustard, although it takes at least 1 quart of seeds to make a single jar.

Growing Guide

Shade 1 to 3. Sow seeds thickly in early spring or midsummer. Thin by pulling plants (which can be eaten) or use a knife or scissors to cut small leaves about $1/2$ inch from the ground as salad fixings and then regrow.

Species, Varieties, Cultivars and Hybrids

B. juncea var. *rugosa*. Mustard can be grown as a tall ground-cover or intermixed in borders. The handsome red-veined leaves are highly decorative. Leave space when planting, for the plants eventually grow 3 feet tall with an equal spread. Zones 7 to 9.

Browallia

Amethyst flower

These intensely blue flowers are seldom seen in six-packs, so look for seeds in nurseries and catalogs. Browallia grows during the warm summer months, so start them in the ground when you set in tomatoes or other warm weather crops. Sow them in drifts for large splashes of color in the woodland garden. They also grow well in

Pak choi is one of the vegetables that can tolerate some shade.

SHRUBS

Shrubs can be considered the "half walls" that anchor everything else in the garden, falling, as they do in mid-view, from knee height to eye level. There are worlds of shrubs to choose from: quick-growing shrubs like pittosporums to create a private view, shrubs like rhododendrons that burst into bloom with candelabras of flowers or shrubs like lilac that send out waves of perfume while they are in flower. Shrubs come with variegated leaves like hydrangea or the bright red foliage of photinia, bursting out in the early spring. Once you determine what you need, there is a shrub to fit the purpose. On the following pages you'll also find a few shrubs that

grow tall enough to be considered small trees once they are pruned appropriately.

Most shrubs are quite pest free, although some will fall prey to mildew or to an infestation of spider mites or aphids. Keep your shrubs as healthy as possible by feeding them regularly; for mild winter climates, fertilize in the fall and in cold winter climates fertilize in the spring. Use an all-purpose, time-release fertilizer according to the instructions. If you have acid-loving shrubs, such as rhododendrons, azaleas and camellias, use an acid-forming fertilizer (such as aluminum sulfate). Mulching with pine needles and oak leaves is another way to increase the acidity of the soil.

pots, and will overwinter in a warm greenhouse.

Growing Guide

Shade 1 to 2. Sow seeds in early spring for long summer bloom.

Species, Varieties, Cultivars and Hybrids

Browallia americana. Grows 1 to 2 feet high. Covered with light blue or violet flowers.

B. speciosa. A perennial variety growing up to 24 to 30 inches tall. Survives mild winters. Purple star-like flowers bloom depending upon the season they were sown. Zone 10.

Buddleia

Buddleia, butterfly bush

Butterflies flutter around the lilac-look-alike blossoms that open in midsummer in tones of purple, white, pink or blue. The long tapering leaves are

Boxwood.

dark green on top, mossy white underneath. The shrub shoots up to 10 feet tall with rapid growth in the spring. It may die down to the roots during winter, but regrows the next spring.

Growing Guide

Shade 1. Needs at least 2 hours of direct sun a day. Water infrequently. Mulch heavily before the first frost. If the stems die back during winter, fertilize in the spring and move mulch back from around the base.

Species, Varieties, Cultivars and Hybrids

B. davidii 'Black Knight'. Up to 15 feet with dark purple flowers. Zones 5 to 9.

B. d. 'Harlequin'. Variegated foliage and purple flowers. Zones 5-9.

B. d. 'Peace'. Up to 15 feet with white blooms. Zones 5 to 9.

B. d. 'Royal Red'. Up to 15 feet with deep pinky purple flowers. Zones 5 to 9.

Buxus

Boxwood

Although it grows slowly, boxwood can be purchased in

1- or 5-gallon containers to get a jump on growing hedges or evergreen accents in the shade garden. Boxwood is very shade tolerant; once established, it can be drought tolerant as well. The small shrub can be shaped into topiary forms. The French often used boxwood in their formal gardens to outline geometrically shaped beds. Its tight shape makes it less useful in the woodland garden.

Growing Guide

Set out boxwood at any time of year. Because boxwood grows so slowly, do not set plants too far apart when planting a hedge as it may take years to fill in. Prune as needed if you are using boxwood in a formal hedge. Prune yearly after spring growth for a less formal hedge.

Species, Varieties, Cultivars and Hybrids

B. microphylla japonica. Grows slightly more vigorously than the Korean boxwood and is hardy to -10°F. Zones 6 to 9.

B. microphylla koreana. A hardy variety with smaller leaves than Japanese boxwood. Zones 6 to 9.

Buddleia davidii, *butterfly bush.*

C-D

Fancy-leafed caladiums.

Caladium

Fancy-leafed caladium

A tuberous-rooted perennial for the variegated garden or simply in pots as an accent, caladiums are valued for their leaves, not their flowers. Plants grow from tubers to an average height of 2 feet. There are white and green types, as well as blotched red and pink. Start the plants from bulbs or purchase growing plants from nurseries. This tropical plant wants warm temperatures of at least 70°F.

Growing Guide

Shade 1 to 3. Grow caladium as you would tuberous begonias, but plant with the knobby side of the bulb facing up. When the tuber sprouts, plant it in a container, covering it with 2 inches of potting mix. Feed heavily once leaves emerge and begin to grow. Keep the air moist by misting or suspending the container on top of a pebble-filled saucer filled with water. To plant in the ground, fill a planting hole with potting mix and plant the tuber as above. Make sure to feed heavily through the growing season. In the fall, gradually reduce moisture, lift tubers and store with your other bulbs. It can be left in the ground in Zone 10.

Species, Varieties, Cultivars and Hybrids

C. bicolor. Grows 2 to 4 feet tall with large 1-foot-long leaves. Don't let evening temperatures fall below 60°F.

Caltha

Marsh marigold

Marsh marigold is a deciduous, perennial bog plant growing along the edges of streams or lakes. Use marsh marigold to ring your bog area. The bright yellow flowers and the bright glossy-green foliage look well teamed with ferns and water-loving iris.

Growing Guide

Shade 1 to 3. Choose a location where the roots of the marsh marigold can stay moist. Start it in spring and by June you will be able to take divisions to increase your stock.

In southern areas, caladiums are hardy. But elsewhere the tubers need to be dug each winter.

Caladium.

Species, Varieties, Cultivars and Hybrids

C. palustris. Grows vigorously as long as the roots stay moist. Yellow flowers can be 2 inches wide, and the plant grows up to 2 feet tall. Zones 4 to 9.

Camellia
Camellia

Don't pass up camellias just because you live in a cold winter area. There are many new hardier hybrids such as 'Donation', 'Polar Ice', 'Winter's Charm' and 'Winter's Waterlily' that have been bred to withstand cold. So check with your local nursery to see what might be available. Camellias star in the shade garden, their bright glossy green leaves polka-dotted with blooms in colors from pure white to pinks and reds and variegated types. Make an effort to actually see the plant in bloom before you purchase it as there are countless different blossom shapes, colors and sizes. Choose different varieties for a succession of bloom from late winter to late spring. Plant camellias under canopy trees, espalier the open-growing types against a wall or show off slow-growing types in containers. Dense-growing

varieties, such as *C. japonica* and its hybrids can be clipped into a hedge, perfect for creating a shady avenue.

Growing Guide

Shade 1 to 3 depending upon variety. Gardeners in cold winter areas can grow camellias in containers, moving them indoors to a protected spot in winter. Camellias prefer acid soil, consistent moisture during the growing season and an acid-based fertilizer sparsely provided (best at half the recommended dosage) for the first three months of the growing season. Prune only to shape, just after blooming. Once established, some camellias are remarkably drought tolerant. Without sufficient shade, they will sunburn, especially if exposed to hot, direct sun. You can prune older bushes into multiple-stemmed small trees.

Species, Varieties, Cultivars and Hybrids

As you would imagine with such a beloved shrub, there are many varieties and cultivars to choose from—including more hardy varieties for the warmest of northern gardens. These are the main types.

Camellias have a distinctive, elegant appeal.

C. japonica. The most widely known variety. Blooms from early winter into late spring. Dense growth. Zones 7 to 9.

C. reticulata. Very large flowers grow on open, lank branches. Good for espalier or vine treatment. Zones 9 to 10.

C. sasanqua. The earliest blooming with open fragile flowers that may be fragrant. These take the most sun if well watered. Zones 7 to 9.

Camellia japonica *'Pearl Maxwell'.*

'Royal Velvet' camellia has a rich, dark color.

Campanula
Bellflower

A large family with countless varieties showing off bell-shaped blooms in colors from white to shades of blue. Some are drought tolerant while others prefer constant moisture, but all grow well in the shade or part shade. Grow bellflowers as a groundcover in a lath house or choose the vining types to tumble down the sides of a hanging container. Some grow in a miniature scale suited to rock gardens. Many are perennials, while some grow as biennials.

Growing Guide

Shade 1 to 3. Plant out in early spring in a shady spot such as under shrubs or in shady borders. Prune back perennials after blooming to encourage repeat bloom. Water consistently. Divide clumps of perennials when they begin to diminish in bloom or crowd their planting area.

Species, Varieties, Cultivars and Hybrids

C. carpatica, Tussock bellflower. A compact plant useful in the front of borders or in rock gardens. Grows up to 1 1/2 feet tall. Zones 4 to 8.

C. medium, Canterbury bell, cup-and-saucer plant. This biennial grows up to 4 feet tall with blue, pink or white bell-shaped flowers. A striking flowering plant. Zones 5 to 8.

C. rotundifolia, Bluebell of Scotland. Up to 2 feet tall with blue, 1-inch-wide bells. Good under trees in a woodland setting, where they may resow. Zones 4 to 8.

Campsis
Trumpet creeper

The bright orange, trumpet-shaped blooms of campsis seem to glow in the shade garden. Deciduous, in the spring it bursts forth with leaves that are followed by bright blooms from late summer into fall. It can grow to the unwieldy height of 40 feet or more, although in the shade it is more contained.

Growing Guide

Shade 1 to 2. Introduce this vine to a large space it can fill up, such as an area you might want quickly screened. It climbs with sticky rootlet feet, so it is difficult to persuade it to leave after it becomes attached. It will spread like a blackberry through its suckering roots, shooting up and away from the original

Trumpet creeper is very attractive to hummingbirds. Some people even call it the hummingbird vine.

Chamaecyparis.

plant. Prune vigorously while dormant.

Species, Varieties, Cultivars and Hybrids

C. grandiflora, Chinese trumpet vine. Does not grow as large as *C. radicans*. Has larger, bright scarlet-orange flowers. Zones 7 to 9.

C. radicans. Originally an Eastern United States native, *C. radicans* withstands cold temperatures. If it freezes back, it will reshoot in the spring. Vigorous growth to 40-plus feet. *C. r.* 'Flava' has golden flowers. Zones 5 to 9.

Chamaecyparis
False cypress

A slow-growing dwarf conifer suitable for small gardens, this plant shows remarkable variety. Excellent for introducing a variety of forms into the shade garden.

Growing Guide

Shade 1 to 3. Plant false cypress in the shade, making sure to water regularly until you see new growth. If two leaders appear, prune back to one to assure good shape to the plant.

Species, Varieties, Cultivars and Hybrids

C. obtusa 'Crippsii'. Stringy bark and aromatic bright golden yellow foliage. Upright columnar growth to 20 feet.

C. o. 'Nana Gracilis'. A dwarf form that grows only to 4 feet tall. Zones 6 to 8.

Cimicifuga
Bugbane

A dramatic plant for the shade garden, with white flowering plumes rising up above the shade border. The leaves are fern-like, with a delicate, finely cut appearance. Use the taller varieties in the back of the border, or mix them with ferns in a woodland garden. Most start to bloom in midsummer and continue to autumn, filling in what is often a gap in bloom in the garden. Match bugbane with astilbe or Japanese anemone for great late summer bloom.

Growing Guide

Shade 1 to 3. Bugbane likes a rich, moist soil that drains, so don't use the plant in a bog situation. As the plant matures, it forms large clumps which should not be disturbed. If you need to divide the clumps, do so in spring before new foliage develops. In mild winter areas, divide the clumps in fall. Zones 4 to 8.

Species, Varieties, Cultivars and Hybrids

C. japonica. A medium-sized plant just 3 to 4 feet tall with white blooms.

C. racemosa. One of the tallest, with spikes towering to 7 feet.

C. simplex 'White Pearl'. Large flower spikes.

Claytonia
Spring beauty

Although you may have some problem finding this locally, and have to resort to mail-order to find it, this is a useful plant for the garden. In earliest spring, small clumps of foliage appear, followed by icy-pink blooms. By summer the plant has disappeared from the border, leaving room for other summer blooming plants to spread.

Growing Guide

Shade 1 to 3. Plant in the fall toward the front of the border so the 12-inch clump doesn't get lost. Mass together underneath deciduous shrubs which cover with leaves during the summer.

Species, Varieties, Cultivars and Hybrids

C. virginica. A perennial forming clumps of 4-inch-high plants with a 6-inch spread. Look for pink blooms in early spring. Zones 6 to 8.

Claytonia virginica.

Clematis has been called queen of the flowering vines.

Clematis have flowers in shades of red and pink, as well as white and yellow.

when plants bloom: prune spring-blooming types after blooming for they blossom on the previous year's wood; prune summer- and fall-blooming plants late in the fall as they bloom on each spring's growth. Unlike many shade plants, clematis does not like acid soil, so keep soil neutral. Mulch the roots to keep them cool. Water consistently.

Species, Varieties, Cultivars and Hybrids

C. armandii, Evergreen clematis. White spring flowers are richly fragrant with hints of

Clematis

Clematis

The number of clematis varieties and cultivars is nothing short of overwhelming. Their blooms can be remarkable for their size or their profusion. And some types, if pruned after the spring bloom, repeat later in the summer. All need consistent moisture and cool roots, so mulch them heavily. Plant clematis underneath a climbing rose and let the vine lean on the rose for support. Clematis makes a superb choice for an arbor or pergola. There is an evergreen type with vanilla-fragrant blooms in early spring.

Growing Guide

Shade 1 to 2. Plant in a location where there is support for the stems because clematis needs something to twine around. Prune according to

White-flowering clematis tend to show the most in shady areas.

vanilla. Quickly grows to 20 feet. 'Henderson Rubra' blooms in pink flowers. Prune heavily after blooming to keep branches from tangling. Zones 5 to 9.

Clivia
Kaffir lily

Clumps of brightly flowered orange clivia are a staple of landscapes in mild winter climates. But if protected, this South African bulb will bloom in March and April in cooler areas. Clivia wants no direct sun and regular watering. Grow clivia in containers in cold winter areas and overwinter in a protected location.

Growing Guide

Shade 2 to 3. Plant clivia with the top of the tuber just above the ground level. Do not disturb either in containers or in the ground, for the roots prefer to be crowded. Mix in borders with ferns, rhododendrons and azaleas that coordinate with the orange or yellow flowers. Watch for slugs and snails feasting on the succulent leaves. Zone 10.

Species, Varieties, Cultivars and Hybrids

C. miniata, Kaffir lily. Strap-like leaves rise to 2 feet. The bloom stalk, heavy with bright orange flowers, rises up from the middle of the fan of leaves.

The flowers of sweet autumn clematis have an exquisite fragrance.

Clivia miniata.

Colchicum
Autumn crocus

Colchicums are fall-blooming bulbs that, like the naked ladies, send out strap-shaped leaves first, which die back before the flowers appear. Like magic, in the fall, colchicum blossoms spring up in shades of white and pink. Place the low-blooming flowers in the front of borders and planting beds, figuring on some period with large clumps of somewhat unbeautiful, strappy leaves. All parts of this bulb are poisonous.

Growing Guide

Shade 1 and 2. Plant colchicum when they are dormant in July or August, 4 to 5 inches under the soil. Do not disturb; if you want to divide clumps, dig only in the dormant period.

Species, Varieties, Cultivars and Hybrids

C. autumnale, meadow saffron. Naked stems with pink trumpet-

For moist shady areas, nothing looks more tropical than elephant's ear.

like flowers follow the spring growth of strap-like leaves. Zones 5 to 9.

C. speciosum, 'The Giant'. A single light purple, or *C.* 'Waterlily', a double. Zones 6 to 9.

Colocasia
Elephant's ear, taro root

The plant for a tropical bog garden, or planted in a container kept continuously moist, an elephant's ear is sure to put on a show. The large and impressive leaves grow to 3 or $3^{1}/_{2}$ feet, and the taro (roots) are edible. Elephant's ear is very tender, so protect the plants as temperatures drop in the fall.

Growing Guide

Shade 1 to 2. Plant the tubers in a rich, moist, shady location in the spring after all danger of frost has passed. Keep the soil moist. Dig tubers before frost in the fall and, after drying, store them in perlite or sawdust in a cool, dry place.

Species, Varieties, Cultivars and Hybrids

C. esculenta, elephant's ear, taro root. Large, heart-shaped leaves make a green statement planted in a bog or clustered in large containers. Dramatic in a small water container all by itself. Zones 9 to 10.

Colchicums, like some crocus, send up showy flowers in autumn.

Lily-of-the-valley flowers have a delicate fragrance and red, poisonous fruits.

The flowering dogwood is a favorite small tree.

Convallaria
Lily-of-the-valley

The hanging, white, bell-shaped flowers of lily-of-the-valley are beloved for their fragrance and dainty blooms. Lily-of-the-valley spreads out to make a carpet of light green leaves under shade-loving shrubs or tall trees.

Growing Guide

Shade 1 to 2. Plant out in the fall before the first frost. Plant them 2 inches deep with each pip spaced about 4 inches apart. Cover them with a rich mulch every year.

Species, Varieties, Cultivars and Hybrids

C. majalis. Grows 9 to 12 inches with bright green leaves and sprays of early spring bell-like blooms. Naturalizes and spreads to make a green carpet. Zones 4 to 9.

Cornus
Dogwood

A beloved group of shrubs and small trees with white, pink or red flowers in spring followed by white, purple or red fruits. Some have autumn foliage displays, others have brightly colored branches during the winter, while still others have distinct bark or spectacular fruits. Many gardeners don't consider it spring until the dogwood trees bloom. Look for the

Flowering dogwood.

classic combination of dogwood, azalea and rhododendron for an explosion of woodland color to make you forget the winter blues.

Growing Guide

Shade 1 or 2. Most dogwoods are happy in light shade with a moist soil that's slightly acidic. Make sure dogwoods have plenty of moisture during the summer growing season. They make fine specimen trees or shrubs, or are great in groups or woodland gardens.

Species, Varieties, Cultivars and Hybrids

C. alternifolia, pagoda dogwood. A small tree or large shrub with small white flowers and purple fruits. The tree has a very horizontal spreading form. Grows 25 feet tall and wide. Zones 4 to 8.

C. florida, eastern dogwood. Growing to 40 feet, the eastern dogwood heralds spring with white blossoms. There are pink and red cultivars. *C. f.* 'Welchii' has variegated leaves of pink, red, deep rose and green. Zones 5 to 9.

C. mas, cornelian cherry. A shrub to 12 feet tall with creamy flowers in spring. There are several variegated cultivars such as 'Pioneer', 'Red Star' and 'Variegata'. Zones 4 to 8.

C. nuttallii, Pacific dogwood. Native to the West Coast and growing up to 50 feet tall and 20 feet wide, the Pacific dogwood blooms in spring with white or pink blossoms followed by red fruits and autumn color. Zones 7 to 9.

Cornelian cherry.

English hawthorn in bloom.

Crataegus
Hawthorn
A fully hardy, small deciduous tree that fits in well just about anywhere, hawthorn is unfussy about shade, drought and soil. Choose types such as *C. viridis* that are less susceptible to fireblight to decrease incidence. Hawthorns display pink or white flowers in the spring followed by clusters of red fruits that attract birds. Some types even have fall color.

English hawthorn.

Growing Guide
Shade 1 to 2. Not recommended as a patio tree for aphids can be a seasonal problem, dripping sticky honeydew on tables and chairs. Do not overwater or overfertilize as the new growth is more susceptible to fireblight.

Species, Varieties, Cultivars and Hybrids
C. x carrierei, Lavelle hawthorn. White flowers in the spring with large berries. Leaves turn in the fall. Zones 5 to 7.

C. laevigata, English hawthorn. A smaller hawthorn, 18 to 20 feet tall with a spreading canopy. 'Paul's Scarlet' bears red flowers, 'Double Pink' has double pink flowers. Zones 5 to 7.

Crataegus phaenopyrum.

C. phaenopyrum, firethorn. A 30-foot native with white flowers and brilliant red fruits in winter. Zones 4 to 7.

C. viridis, green hawthorn. White flowers in the spring cover this 25- to 30-foot-tall tree. One of the least susceptible to fireblight. Zones 5 to 7.

Crinum
Crinum
These old-fashioned bulbs are still widely available but not well known. Beloved for decades, crinum make large spear-shaped leaf clumps that fill the shade border with green texture. In late summer, tall, lily-like blooms in white or pink appear suspended on tall stems. The fragrance of this long-lasting flower is exquisite. Place crinum at the back of borders, along a narrow bed or in a line underneath shrubs or small trees.

Growing Guide
Shade 1. Plant bulbs 6 inches under the soil's surface. Keep as moist as possible. Protect from cold temperatures. Can be grown with less water, although its appearance becomes ragged. The bulbs are tender at 20°F, but can be heavily mulched and

Crinum *x powellii 'Album'.*

Crinum moorei.

Crocus vernus.

survive down to 10°F. Lift bulbs to overwinter indoors in colder climates.

Species, Varieties, Cultivars and Hybrids

C. moorei. Pinkish red flowers. Zones 8 to 10.

C. x. *powellii* 'Album'. White flowers. Zones 6 to 10.

Crocus

Crocus

Beloved in the early spring garden, hybrid crocus are widely available. Experiment with species crocus (the very earliest to spring up) and fall crocus (that light up the autumn garden). The flowers are small, so plant them in masses where they will not be obscured. Remember—this is one of the

squirrel's favorite spring foods, and both blossoms and bulbs are fodder for their pantries.

Growing Guide

Plant the bulbs where they receive winter or spring sun but with shade all summer long—the perfect spot is under deciduous trees. Crocus will reseed themselves as they naturalize.

Species, Varieties, Cultivars and Hybrids

C. sativus, saffron crocus. The source of saffron, the stamens of this small purple bloom are

Crocus vernus.

collected for culinary use. Blooms in the fall. Zones 6 to 9.

C. speciosus, showy crocus. Fall-blooming. Zones 5 to 9.

C. tommasinianus, 3 to 6 inches high. Zones 5 to 8.

Cucumis

Cucumber

All the books tell you to grow cucumbers in full sun, but they grow successfully with just 4 hours of sun a day. Try small varieties like gherkins to grow in hanging containers or on a patio with morning sun. Let the cucumber crawl across the warm surface of the patio to spur on fruiting.

Growing Guide

Shade 1. Choose varieties that ripen quickly, called early season varieties. Start the seeds indoors 6 weeks before the last frost, or plant them directly in the ground when the soil has warmed. Make sure they receive 4 hours of direct sunlight a day. Train them up a trellis or let them sprawl on the ground. Try growing them in a large container. Mulch well.

Species, Varieties, Cultivars and Hybrids

Early season varieties such as 'Picklebush' are best.

Cucumber 'Spacemaster'.

Cyclamen
Hardy cyclamen

Most gardeners know the florist variety of cyclamen sold during the dreary end of winter, so capable of dressing up the indoors with their bright pink, purple, red or white butterfly-shaped blossoms. Hardy cyclamens, however, naturalize well outdoors in the shade. Smaller than the florist variety, they make a charming display under shrubs or in a woodland setting. Even when they are out of bloom, the heart-shaped leaves look clean and crisp. There are early spring, summer and fall-blooming varieties.

Growing Guide

Shade 2 to 3. Set the tubers into rich, moist humus soil during their dormancy, June through August. Cover the bulbs with just $^1/_2$ inch of soil. Let the bulbs stay undisturbed.

Species, Varieties, Cultivars and Hybrids

C. coum, Atkin's cyclamen. Purple-pink blooms. Zones 5 to 8.

C. hederifolium, sometimes sold as *C. neapolitanum*. Happy in the dry summer shade garden, the plant boasts variegated leaves that look like they have been splashed with silver paint. Blooms are pink or white. Don't forget that plants go dormant in July or August—meaning they are not dead. Zones 5 to 9.

Cypripedium
Pink lady's slipper

A fully hardy terrestrial orchid that blooms after a deciduous period in the spring or early summer. The pouched lip is pink with darker veins. Do not to try to transplant these from the wild; instead purchase propagated plants from a reputable nursery.

Growing Guide

Shade 2 to 3. Plant in a moist location with soil well-enriched with organic ingredients. Mark the site as the plant totally disappears over winter. Water consistently so the soil does not dry out. Fertilize lightly in the fall in mild winter areas or in the spring in colder locations.

Species, Varieties, Cultivars and Hybrids

C. acaule, pink lady's slipper. Bright green 4- to 10-inch-long leaves emerge in the spring followed by the 2-inch-long bloom in late spring. Zones 5 to 8.

Daffodils (See Narcissus)

Daphne
Daphne

A small shrub that tolerates shade as long as it receives at least 2 hours of direct sun a day. The small pink flowers are harbingers of early spring and pack a punch of perfume. The tidy, glossy leaves and slow growth to 5 feet makes daphne easy to incorporate into any garden. Daphne also works well as a container plant.

Growing Guide

Shade 1. Provide at least 2 hours of direct sun. Once planted, daphne doesn't like to be disturbed, so try not to move it. The roots rot easily if the soil doesn't drain perfectly. Mulch well and provide consistent summer moisture. Feed the plants in the late fall to stimulate spring bloom.

Species, Varieties, Cultivars and Hybrids

D. alpina. A dwarf variety excellent in rock gardens with gray-green leaves. Zones 6 to 8.

Cyclamen coum.

Winter-flowering daphne is an especially fragrant shrub.

D. odora. An evergreen shrub to 5 feet tall. Covered with clusters of fragrant flowers in early spring. *D. o.* 'Aureomarginata' has variegated leaves with the edges lined in yellow. Zones 6 to 7.

Dicentra

Bleeding heart

An old favorite of Victorian gardens, the bleeding heart—with its ferny foliage and rows of heart-shaped blooms hanging off leafless stems almost horizontally—is a shade garden staple. They like consistent moisture and rich soil. Take care in using some kinds because they go dormant in summer.

Growing Guide

Plant out roots in earliest spring in humus-rich soil. If you prune off dead flower stems, you may have a repeat bloom. Mark their site as some disappear when they go dormant in midsummer. Pair with ferns and surround with summer annuals to fill in as the plants go dormant. Keep the soil moist.

Species, Varieties, Cultivars and Hybrids

D. eximia 'Luxuriant', fringed bleeding heart. Clumps to $1^1/2$ feet high with deep pink flowers. White form is 'Alba' and numerous other hybrids have longer blooming seasons. Does not go dormant.

D. spectabilis, common bleeding heart. Clumps grow to 2 to 3 feet. Large, 1-inch flowers hang from stems in mid-spring. Zones 3 to 8.

Dicksonia

Tree fern

The tree ferns look like a cross between a miniature palm tree and a gigantic fern. The graceful fronds top a furry, reddish trunk 3 to 6 feet tall. At home in the shade, they work as well underneath a tall conifer as they do in an alley along a pathway. A forest of tree ferns is magical. Try them as the centerpiece of a subtropical garden. Grown as a container plant, they can overwinter in a protected spot in cold winter regions.

Growing Guide

Shade 1 to 3. Grow these gentle giants as you would ordinary ferns. Although they are slow-growing, they are gracious in any warm weather garden. Prune off fronds as they die

Whether in containers or in topical areas, tree ferns are dramatic.

back in summer. Plant them in containers in locations where the temperature drops under 20°F so you can move them under cover for protection.

Species, Varieties, Cultivars and Hybrids

D. antarctica, Tasmanian tree fern. An evergreen fern that grows as a small—up to 12 feet—tree. The new fronds uncurl from the center. The trunks are covered in a furry fiber. The most common and the most hardy of all the tree ferns. The Tasmanian tree fern withstands temperatures down to 20°F. Zones 9 to 10.

FERNS

A staple of wooded forest floors, boggy creeksides and even dry shady cliffs, ferns are an ancient plant, evolving eons ago in a larger form as, believe it or not, fodder for vegetarian dinosaurs. A coveted find of rock hunters are ancient ferns pressed permanently into rocks. Yet even today, although shrunken in size from dinosaur days, the ferns' delicate forms and beautifully textured leaves add immeasurably to the shade garden. Many are hardy enough to survive winters as far north as Minnesota or the upper peninsula of Michigan with its sub-zero temperatures; others live un-thirstily through a dry California summer. Find the ferns that suit your environment and enjoy their ancient beauty.

Digitalis purpurea *'Foxy'*.

D. purpurea 'Shirley'. Grows to 6 feet tall. Gracious bloom stalks bear spikes of tubular flowers in a range of pinks and purples. Place in the back of the shady border.

D. p. 'Foxy'. The smallest of the digitalis (to only 3 feet) can be relegated to the front of the shady border. It is used as an annual, blooming six months after sowing. Reseeds.

Doronicum
Leopard's bane

A daisy-like flowering perennial for the shady cutting garden from early to midspring. Growing in clumps, leopard's bane sends up 2-inch flowers in shades of yellow. The plant is up to 3 feet tall and the leaves offer an attractive heart shape.

Growing Guide

Most leopard's bane plants die back in midsummer, so interplant them with summer annuals to cover their disappearance. Mark their location and provide consistent moisture during their dormancy. Divide the clumps every 2 years as the younger plants provide more blooms.

Digitalis
Foxglove

Big, soft fuzzy-leaved plants topped by a tall bloom stalk with trumpet-shaped flowers make this one of the tallest citizens of the shade border, up to 5 feet. Although comparable to delphiniums, foxglove looks like a wild woodland plant and self-sows happily. Foxglove makes a splendid display along a shady border or scattered amidst trees and ferns. Although most of the blooms come in late spring, remove the bloom stalk and smaller blooms will occur farther down through the summer. Hummingbirds hover over the blossoms.

Growing Guide

Shade 1 to 3. Digitalis is a biennial, so plant in late fall. Watch out for slugs and snails which can devour a young plant overnight. Let last blooms set seed and scatter for new plants. Digitalis will take some drought although it looks lusher with water. Zones 4 to 8.

Species, Varieties, Cultivars and Hybrids

D. grandiflora. A true perennial foxglove with 2-foot spikes of soft, pale yellow flowers.

Many foxgloves are biennial, but some are perennial, like D. grandiflora.

Digitalis.

Species, Varieties, Cultivars and Hybrids

D. cordatum 'Magnificent' bears larger flowers on 1¹/₂-foot stems. Zones 4 to 8.

D. plantagineum, plaintain leopard's bane. Larger leaves with 3-foot-tall stems showing off 2- to 4-inch-wide flowers. Excellent for the dry shade garden. Zones 5 to 8.

Drimys
Winter's bark

An excellent evergreen patio tree, winter's bark grows up to 40 feet with fragrant star-shaped flowers. The green, glossy leaves are ovoid. Winter's bark mixes well with rhododendrons with the similarity of their leaf shape and the shared requirements of rich, moist soil.

Growing Guide

Shade 1 to 2. It is rather frost hardy, but best grown in a protected location in cold winter areas. Mulch the roots heavily.

Species, Varieties, Cultivars and Hybrids

D. winteri, winter's bark. An evergreen tree with clusters of white star-shaped fragrant flowers borne in early summer. Zones 9 to 10.

Dryopteris erythrosora
Wood fern

The wood fern is native in most forests in America and some around the world. Hardy and resilient when given moist and rich soil, it makes a great filler in the woodland gardens and in shade borders. Indispensible for an all-green garden.

Growing Guide

Shade 2 to 3. Check the local conditions of your regional wood fern and be sure to follow them. One California wood fern, *D. arguta,* will not tolerate over-watering in the dry summers, while those in other regions benefit from regular summer waterings.

Species, Varieties, Cultivars and Hybrids

D. erythrosora, Japanese shield fern. As the new fronds appear on this evergreen fern, they shine in pinky bronze colors. Mature fronds are about 2 feet long and in a lime green color. Zones 5 to 8.

D. expansa, spreading wood fern. Native to much of America.

Duchesnea
Indian strawberry, mock strawberry

Looking just like a strawberry plant sending out runners that help it spread, this ground-hugging perennial blooms with small yellow flowers followed by tasteless replicas of strawberries.

Foxgloves come in many colors. Many shade gardeners prefer white.

Growing Guide

Shade 1 to 3. Set out plants in moist, rich soil 4 inches apart. For the thickest cover, do not let the soil dry out.

Species, Varieties, Cultivars and Hybrids

D. indica, syn. *Fragaria indica,* Indian strawberry. Mock strawberry forms a low groundcover that grows 4 inches tall. *D. i.* 'Harlequin' has variegated foliage. Zones 5 to 9.

Dryopteris austriaca intermedia.

E-F

Elaeagnus
Russian olive

Among its admirable traits, this small deciduous tree sends out a powerful fragrance from its extremely tiny flowers; its bark shreds for winter interest, while the long lance-shaped leaves are graceful and willow-like. And as a drought-tolerant small shrubby tree, it does well in a dry shade garden.

Growing Guide
Shade 1 to 2. Accepts part shade and needs little watering during the dry months.

Species, Varieties, Cultivars and Hybrids
E. angustifolia, Russian olive. Grows to 20 feet making it suitable for the small garden. Deciduous, the grayish 2-inch leaves are thin and graceful. Powerfully fragrant, tiny flowers. Zones 2 to 9.

Winter aconite naturalized.

Endymion, syn. *Hyacinthoides*
Wood hyacinth

Easy and successful shade bulbs that are fully hardy. The only thing complicated about them is their classification. You may find them listed as squills, under the name *Scilla campanulata* or *Scilla hispanica.* The fragrant blue, bell-like flowers burst out in spring, and can be used inside as cut flowers.

Growing Guide
Shade 1 to 2. Growing 8 to 15 inches tall, the plants naturalize into clumps that should be divided every 5 years. Perfect for the shaded woodland garden or border. Plant them within a low ground cover for a vertical display of foliage and bloom.

Species, Varieties, Cultivars and Hybrids
E. non-scripta or S*cilla non-scripta,* English bluebell. Fragrant and dainty, spreading in blue carpets through the spring garden. The multiple blue, bell-like flowers grow up stems. The foliage is a clump of $^{1}/_{2}$-inch-wide strap leaves. Zones 5 to 8.

Winter aconite.

Eranthis
Winter aconite

Hardy and persistent; winter snows don't seem to bother this yellow-blooming bulb. The stalkless, yellow cup with a ruffle of green petals sits low to the ground. Only about 4 inches tall, winter aconite should be placed in the front of borders. Aconite naturalizes well in woodland gardens.

Growing Guide
Shade 1 to 3. Plant in the front of borders or under deciduous trees in the fall.

Species, Varieties, Cultivars and Hybrids

E. hymenalis, winter aconite. A small buttercup-like flowering plant suited for shade. Make a woodland landscape in early spring dotted with yellow blooms. Zones 4 to 9.

Erythronium
Dog-tooth violet, trout lily

The trout lily is a better description of this charming small plant with its spring bloom. Like tiny miniature lilies, the dainty blooms should be in a prominent spot next to paths or alone under deciduous trees.

Growing Guide

Shade 1 to 2. Plant in moist, rich soil as bulbs or plants. Mulch well.

Species, Varieties, Cultivars and Hybrids

E. dens-canis, dog-tooth violet. Blooms are white, pink and purple. Zones 3 to 8.

E. 'Pagoda', pagoda trout lily. Light yellow flowers. Zones 4 to 8.

Many kinds of dog-tooth violet have delightfully variegated foliage.

Trout lilies have graceful, hanging flowers in shades of yellow, white and pink.

Festuca
Dwarf blue fescue

Small clumps of this blue-gray grass make pointed accents in a shady border, or around rocks in a Japanese-style garden. The blue foliage lights up a shady border.

Growing Guide

Shade 1 to 2. Set clumps in the front to the middle of the border as they may top 12 inches when they mature. Keep the soil moist, and mow or divide the clumps regularly to keep their compact shape. Removing the flowers also helps to keep festuca in good shape.

Species, Varieties, Cultivars and Hybrids

F. ovina glauca, sheep fescue. This dwarf blue fescue grows as a lower growing grass (up to 4 to 12 inches tall) with fine, needle-like leaves. Zones 5 to 8.

Blue fescue.

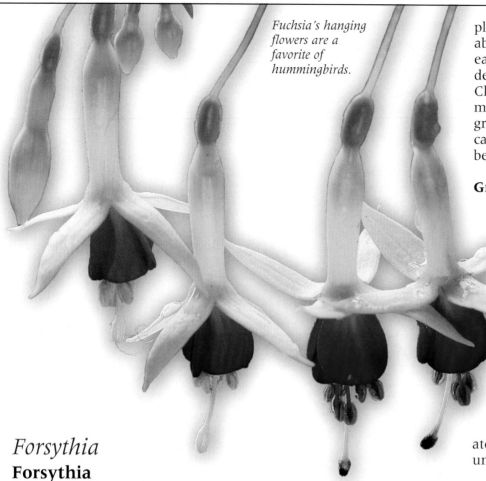

Fuchsia's hanging flowers are a favorite of hummingbirds.

place for them as they are only about 6 to 8 inches tall and can easily be overlooked in the garden's burst of spring bloom. Clustered together they make a more impressive display. They grow easily in containers so you can move them where they will be noticed while in bloom.

Growing Guide

Shade 1 to 2. Plant the bulbs in the fall in an afternoon or morning shaded area in rich, moist soil. Or set out in containers scaled to their diminutive size.

Species, Varieties, Cultivars and Hybrids

F. meleagris, Guinea-hen flower. A spring-flowering bulb that grows 6 to 8 inches high. The checkered blooms atop grassy stems make this an unusual plant. Zones 4 to 8.

Forsythia

Forsythia

Tuck this spring-flowering, deciduous shrub almost anywhere in the garden, even under deciduous trees to bask in the winter sun. In early spring, yellow flowers burst out along the bare branches. Bring the stems into the house and watch the flowers come out. Size varies depending upon variety.

Growing Guide

Shade 1. Forsythia needs at least 2 hours of direct sun daily. Fertilize every fall and prune after bloom by thinning out older branches—all the way to the ground to keep an open untangled look.

Species, Varieties, Cultivars and Hybrids

F. x intermedia 'Beatrix Farrand'. One of the best-known varieties growing to 10 feet tall and 7 feet wide. Zones 5 to 8.

F. ovata, Korean forsythia. The earliest to flower and smaller, only 4 to 6 feet tall and equally wide. Zones 5 to 8.

Fritallaria

Guinea-hen flower, checkered lily

These bulbs with their unusual gingham-checked blooms naturalize in shade gardens. They look like tulips hanging upside down in muted shades of purple and white. Find a special

Fuchsia

Fuchsia

Fuchsias serve many different chores in the garden. The branching types, with their basket-like blossoms dangling over the sides of a hanging

Forsythia is one of the earliest-blooming of the spring-flowering shrubs.

Forsythia flowers are sometimes forced because they appear before the leaves.

container, should be in every lath house—hung high so you look up into their intriguing blossoms. Train the taller growing types as standards or small shrubs. You can espalier some varieties against fences or walls. Although many cold-weather gardeners grow them as annuals, they are perennials in mild winter areas.

Growing Guide

Shade 1 to 3. A denizen of the shade, fuchsias will take some filtered sunlight. They are thirsty plants, needing their soil to be more or less constantly moist and the conditions humid. In dry climates, make sure to suspend the container over a saucer filled with pebbles and water. Fertilize regularly during the summer season and pinch to keep plants bushy and stimulate bloom.

Species, Varieties, Cultivars and Hybrids

There are hundreds of different types with blooms from about $^{1}/_{4}$ inch long to the size of a tennis ball. Blooms are multicolored in shades of red, pink, purple and bicolored with white. Collecting fuchsias becomes addictive.

Fuchsia
Hardy fuchsia, lady's eardrops

Although sometimes described as a shrub, hardy fuchsia grows more like a woody vine with open growth that takes well to being trained along a fence or wall. Covered with long red and purple blooms from summer until the first frost, this plant is the equivalent of a hummingbird's delicatessen.

Growing Guide

Shade 1 to 2. Mulch the roots heavily in fall to help carry the plant over the winter. In the spring, feed well, guiding the emerging stems where you want them. Zones 7 to 8.

Species, Varieties, Cultivars and Hybrids

F. magellanica 'Alba' has pale pink flowers.

Many fuchsias feature hanging flowers in contrasting colors.

The checkered flowers of the Guinea-hen flower are very attractive.

G-K

Galium

Sweet woodruff

In medieval times this woodland herb was added to a wine cup, particularly in the spring; or it was used in the household dried in garlands to sweeten the air. The shiny green circular arrangement of the leaves like spokes around the stem appear like a 'ruff', giving the plant its name. White star-shaped flowers appear in the spring.

Growing Guide

Shade 1 to 2. Provide rich soil, moisture and a shady location. When woodruff finds suitable conditions, it spreads and becomes a useful groundcover 6 to 8 inches tall.

Species, Varieties, Cultivars and Hybrids

G. odoratum. A low ground-cover that spreads readily given moisture and a rich humus soil. Woodruff stays a low 6 to 8 inches with white flowers in spring. Zones 4 to 8.

Galanthus

Snowdrop

One of the earliest spring flowers, galanthus pops up soon after the snow has melted. The cheery white bell-shaped flower (one per stalk) is tipped with green on the

Snowdrops are some of the earliest-flowering spring bulbs.

inside. A good woodland flower under trees or shrubs in areas where drifts of white blossoms can naturalize. Likes moist soil.

Growing Guide

Shade 1 to 2. Plant 4 inches deep in the fall, spacing the

Sweet woodruff flowers smell of freshly mown hay.

bulbs 3 inches apart. Divide rarely and then only just after blooming.

Species, Varieties, Cultivars and Hybrids

G. elwesii, giant snowdrop. Flowering stem grows to 12 inches tall. Zones 3 to 9.

G. nivalis, common snowdrop. Smaller than the giant snowdrop and blooms earlier. Look for 'Double Snowdrop' or 'Flore Pleno'. Zones 3 to 9.

Geranium
Cranesbill

Gardeners tend to mislabel all the cheerful old-fashioned pelargoniums as "geraniums," giving the true geraniums a miss. These perennials do well in the shade and deserve a chance in every shade garden. There are many different sorts, but they all prefer mixed sun and shade, particularly afternoon shade in hot summer areas. Their delicate foliage and long blooming season makes them a good color spot. There are tall types and short types, and their five-petaled flowers come in a variety of colors. The compact forms make good groundcovers or rock garden plants. Their name comes from the seed pod that follows bloom; it looks remarkably like a crane's bill.

Growing Guide

Shade 1 to 2. Plant out geraniums in a lightly shaded spot in early spring or, in mild winter areas, in late fall. Clumps can be left for years, or until blooms begin to diminish. Then divide in the early spring or late fall. Keep plants consistently moist in well-draining soil.

Species, Varieties, Cultivars and Hybrids

G. 'Johnson's Blue' is a striking hybrid with clear blue flowers and deeply divided

Hakonechloa macra *'Aureola'*.

leaves. Grows to 20 inches. Zones 4 to 8.

G. phaeum, mourning widow. Known for its dark purple flowers, this geranium also has nice foliage. A plant for dry shade. Zones 5 to 8.

G. sanguineum, bloody cranesbill. This species has magenta flowers throughout the summer and deeply divided leaves that change color in autumn. Grows to 10 inches. Zones 4 to 8.

Hakonechloa
Japanese forest grass

A variegated green and yellow grass that spreads so slowly, it never becomes invasive. Bloom stalks that are a reddish brown color change the plant's appearance, as if the tips had been dyed. A good candidate for a Japanese garden or a variegated garden. Grows up to 12 inches.

Growing Guide

Shade 1 to 3. Plant out clumps in early spring in rich, moist soil. In the fall spread an acid-balanced fertilizer around the base.

Species, Varieties, Cultivars and Hybrids

H. macra 'Albo variegata', Japanese forest grass. Creamy yellow and green striped grass effective to create light spots in a shade garden. Particularly useful in a woodland garden as it looks grassy but never becomes invasive. Zones 5 to 9.

Hakonechloa macra *'Aureola'*.

Halesia carolina.

Witch-hazels have spidery flowers in autumn or spring.

Halesia
Snowdrop tree

Considered one of the finest of all blooming trees, the mature snowdrop can get large—to 20 to 50 feet depending upon the climate—but does so slowly. It is deciduous, blooming in May, with clusters of bell-shaped, white flowers.

Growing Guide

Shade 1. The snowdrop tree pairs well as a canopy tree for rhododendrons and azaleas, particularly when the lower branches are pruned up to allow light in and to view the flowers from underneath. Not appropriate for a small garden. Prune to a single tree trunk unless you want a large shrub-like appearance.

Species, Varieties, Cultivars and Hybrids

H. carolina, snowdrop tree. A deciduous tree which covers itself in bell-like flowers in the spring. Grows 30 to 40 feet tall with leaves turning yellow in the fall. Zones 5 to 8.

Hamamelis
Witch-hazel

A deciduous shrub with spidery-looking, fragrant flowers appearing on bare branches in autumn or early spring. The colors range from bright yellow to orange shades, so check

Some witch-hazels bloom after they lose their foliage; others bloom before that.

flower color before purchasing. Grows well in part shade as long as it is planted in acid soil. Many different varieties and hybrids, most growing 10 to 12 feet tall, although under favorable circumstances witch-hazel can grow to 20 feet tall. In the fall, the leaves turn brilliant yellow or orange-red depending upon variety.

Growing Guide

Shade 1 to 2. Plant in part shade, provide consistent water and mulch roots. An easy-care plant. Prune after flowering just to shape.

Species, Varieties, Cultivars and Hybrids

H. x *intermedia*. Many different cultivars with bright orange flowers and orange or red fall display. 'Arnold Promise' is one of the best. Zones 5 to 9.

H. *japonica*, Japanese witch-hazel. Yellow flowers and yellow fall leaves. Zones 5 to 9.

H. *mollis*, Chinese witch-hazel. Very fragrant yellow flowers with round leaves that turn yellow in autumn. Zones 5 to 9.

Hedera

Ivy

If there was ever an old standby to shade gardening, it would be ivy—tough enough to survive the darkest corners under stairways and along almost shadowy walls on the north side of a house. Ivy climbs walls, spreads underneath decks, porches and stairways and neatens north-facing walls or gardens with its tidy look. But don't allow the thought of ivy to call up only a dark, three-pointed leaf, for ivy comes in many varieties including purple-leafed, variegated light green and white or yellow. One cultivar, *H. helix* 'Pedata', sports a dainty leaf that looks like a bird's footprint; another, *H. h.* 'Filigran', looks like its frilly leaves have had a permanent.

English ivy is a favorite both indoors and outside in shaded areas.

Growing Guide

Shade 1 to 4. Variegated types generally need more sun than the dark green-leafed varieties. An evergreen, ivy can be destructive climbing walls with hairy feet ... bad for stucco and prying off wood shingles. Kept under control, however, it can add immeasurably to the shade garden. Zones dependent upon variety, from fully hardy to half-hardy. Ivy may take as long as a year to become established, but after that growth is rapid.

Species, Varieties, Cultivars and Hybrids

H. canariensis, Canary Island ivy. Evergreen half-hardy. Zones 9 to 10.

H. helix 'Filigran'. Leaves furled and curled. Zones 7 to 9.

H. h. 'Goldheart'. Zones 8 to 9.

H. h. 'Pedata'. Leaves look like bird's feet. Zones 7 to 9.

H. h. 'Buttercup'. Leaves show light yellow centers with green edges the more sun they get. Zones 8 to 9.

Dark green, trailing ivy contrasts well with light-colored stone structures.

Hedera helix.

Helleborus
Christmas rose

These perennials produce winter flowers that appear to look like single roses. A good woodland groundcover, the hellebore's rich leaves make a tidy appearance under shrubs. Each flower, either singles or borne in clusters, has a bright cast of stamens at its center and can last for months.

Growing Guide

Shade 1 to 3. Plant in rich, moist soil and try not to disturb. It may take them some months to establish; after that they don't want to be moved or divided.

Species, Varieties, Cultivars and Hybrids

H. niger, Christmas rose. Grows up to 1¹/₂ feet tall, with flowers anywhere from Christmas to early spring depending upon the winter climate. 2-inch wide flowers can be white or pinkish white. Zones 5 to 9.

Hemerocallis
Daylily

Daylilies provide reliable bloom in the shade garden, and although the individual flowers only last one day, multitudes of flowers open and shut all during the summer. Group daylilies in clusters of color along the shady border or use them dramatically to edge a long pathway. Dwarf varieties stand up to 14 to 16 inches high while some of the larger daylilies make clumps 6 feet tall and almost as wide. The lily-like flowers come in shades of yellow, orange, salmon, pink and red. Try to choose your daylily while it is in bloom, so

Hellebores bloom in the early spring, sometimes before the snow has melted.

you can be assured of color and blossom type.

Growing Guide

Shade 1 to 3. Some daylilies are partially deciduous, dying

Helleborus niger.

down as the fall frosts begin. Others are evergreen. In the spring, the tender new foliage is particularly susceptible to damage by slugs and snails, as are the just-unfurling blooms. Although well-established clumps can be somewhat drought tolerant, for the best foliage keep soil consistently moist. Divide the clumps in the fall or early spring.

Species, Varieties, Cultivars and Hybrids

H. fulva, common daylily. The old-fashioned variety growing to 6 feet tall. Rarely found in nurseries, but passed along from gardener to gardener. Hardy and reliable. Zones 3 to 9.

H. hybrids. Look for evergreen if living in mild winter climates or deciduous in cold winter areas. The deciduous are exceedingly hardy and go dormant in the winter. Look for initials "SM, AM or HM" indicating awards rewarding the plants for their bloom or growth. Zones 4 to 9.

H. lilio-asphodelus, lemon daylily. An old-fashioned variety growing 3 feet tall, with delicate yellow blossoms early in the spring. The lily is particularly admired for its sweet fragrance. Zones 3 to 9.

Daylily.

Hepatica
Liverleaf

A low-growing perennial well suited to the shade garden but not well known. Flowers rise above the leathery leaves on bloom stalks followed by new foliage. Appearing like a small wildflower, liverleaf works well in a woodland garden with consistently moist soil. Once planted, it doesn't want to have its roots disturbed by cultivation.

Helleborus orientalis.

Growing Guide

Shade 2 to 3. Plant liverleaf in a shady spot amended to make a humus-rich soil. The plants are slow-growing but don't want to be transplanted after they have become established, so pick a permanent site and fill in around them with annuals until they mature. Choose a location where the low-growing plants can be viewed from a path or the edge of a lawn. Liverleaf looks great interplanted with daffodils for a spring show.

Species, Varieties, Cultivars and Hybrids

H. americana. Blue, pink, lilac or white flowers in the early spring, each on a single stem. Plants grow to 3 inches high spreading out 5 inches. Very hardy. Zones 4 to 8.

Hosta.

Hostas are some of the most well known shade garden plants.

well as variegated ones. Use them as groundcovers or in a border.

Growing Guide
Shade 1 to 3. Hostas want rich, moist soil. Snails and slugs can be very destructive to the leaves. Zones 4 to 9.

Species, Varieties, Cultivars and Hybrids
Choose from hundreds of hybrids. Among the groups are:

H. crispula, curled-leaf hosta. Large 7-inch leaves have wavy edges to the margins of the leaf. Free-blooming with early-blooming lavender flowers.

H. hybrids. Many, many choices but look for variegated leaves in cream and green, cool blue-toned leaves or shiny yellow leaves to bring color into the shade garden.

H. plantaginea, fragrant plantain lily. Large, 10-inch-long leaves are bright green, mounding up to 2 feet high. The white flowers are sweetly fragrant.

Some of the hostas with blue leaves are the most slug-resistant. Slugs are a major problem for hostas.

Hosta
Plantain lily
One of the favorite plants for the shade garden because of the beauty of its leaf and the pride of its blooming stalk that rises up above the leaves in a handsome display. There are hundreds of types in many shades of green as

Hyacinthus
Dutch hyacinth
Best known as a bulb to be forced inside; some gardeners display handsome pots of the bulb outside on terraces or patios. Look for a new variety which has more than one blooming candelabra stem.

Growing Guide
Plant these in the fall in the shady border.

Hosta 'Krossa Regal' is a very large hosta.

Hyacinths fill the spring air with their fragrance.

Species, Varieties, Cultivars and Hybrids

Multiflora hyacinths. Blooms with a number of blossom stalks.

H. orientalis, common hyacinth. Bloom stalks can grow up to a foot, covered with bell-shaped fragrant flowers. Colors can be white, pink or shades of blue.

Hydrangea
Hydrangea

The most common variety is the well-known, bold-looking, deciduous shrub dressed with

Some hostas have fragrant flowers in shades of lavender or white.

large leaves and extravagant snowball blossoms in summer. The lacecaps with flattened blossoms are rather like large plates of blooms. Blossoms come in white, pink and blue. Hydrangeas are effective as hedges, as a tall background for smaller shrubs, and even as large container plants. One variety is a climbing vine (see next page) willing to clamber up 30-foot walls.

Growing Guide

Shade 1 to 2. Hydrangeas like part shade and consistent moisture all summer long with at least two hours of direct sun daily. When established, hydrangea's need for summer water diminishes. The flowers bloom on growth from the previous year so never prune in the spring. Protect plants from dying down to the ground due to cold. The color of the blossoms is dependent upon the soil pH: in alkaline soil, plants with pink blossoms deepen in color; in acid soil, the flowers will be brilliant blue.

Species, Varieties, Cultivars and Hybrids

H. macrophylla 'Lacecap'. Flattened

Lacecap hydrangeas offer beautiful, delicate-looking flowers.

blossoms in plants that can be dwarf (up to 3 feet) or full size (6 to 7 feet tall). Look for variegated leaf types such as 'Silver variegated Mariesii'. Zones 6 to 9.

H. quercifolia 'Snow Queen'. Leaves shaped like an oak leaf. Zones 5 to 9.

Hydrangea flowers come in a variety of colors. The color is very pH-sensitive, however.

Hydrangea
Climbing hydrangea

An impressive plant that may be difficult to locate, climbing hydrangea is well worth the effort because of its dramatic spring display of fragrant white blooms. It handsomely clothes walls or fences with good-looking foliage and shade; even a north-facing wall is not a problem. Deciduous, the vine bursts out into shiny green leaves in spring, climbing up by sticky feet to two or three stories high—sometimes 30 feet tall.

Growing Guide

Shade 1, 2 and 3. Make sure to plant the climbing hydrangea where there is room to grow. If using a structure, provide a strong one. Climbing hydrangea prefers an east- or north-facing site, and needs rich, moist soil that drains well. Zones 4 to 7.

Species, Varieties, Cultivars and Hybrids

H. anomala petiolaris syn. *Anomala* subsp. *petiolaris.* The

Hydrangea anomala petiolaris.

climbing hydrangea that can cover the sides of three-story buildings. Produces white, flattened blossoms in spring.

Impatiens
Impatiens

These common bedding plants are a boon to the shade gardener

Impatiens wallerana.

from the end of spring until the first fall frost cuts them down. Although they may overwinter in mild winter gardens, generally they are treated as tender annuals. Widely available as summer blooming starts, blossoms come in shades of pinks, salmon, white and purples; some types are striped.

Growing Guide

Shade 1 to 3. Set them into the garden when all danger of frost has passed, because their watery stems are easily damaged. Their compact form can become leggy by the end of the summer season, so pinch to control. Water regularly. They

Impatiens are one of the best-selling annual plants in the country.

are astoundingly compatible to hanging baskets, upright containers, garden beds or woodland gardens.

Species, Varieties, Cultivars and Hybrids

I. wallerana. Look for both single-flowered or double-flowered types. Dwarf varieties are lower growing; the standard may grow up to 12 inches tall. Double-flowered types are more showy than the single-flowered ones.

Iris
Japanese iris, Japanese flag

These iris love the wet, and you can plant them in a bog garden for glorious blooms as large as 4 inches across in rich, deep colors of purple, pinks, red or white. They produce blooms in late spring to early summer.

Growing Guide

Shade 1 to 2. Set out in the fall or spring where the roots stay wet. A bog makes them happy. You can immerse containers of planted Japanese iris into a pond. Some must have moisture when growing in the spring.

Species, Varieties, Cultivars and Hybrids

I. ensata, Japanese iris, Japanese flag. Look for single or double blossoms types when choosing your plants. Japanese iris are tall, growing up to 4 feet, so place

Jasminum polyanthum.

them where they can make a dramatic statement. Zones 5 to 8.

Iris cristata, crested iris. Low-growing, early-blooming iris with white or blue flowers. Zones 4 to 8.

Jasminum
Pink jasmine

Although most books describe this evergreen vine as needing full sun, it tolerates part shade. Early-spring flowers have a delightful fragrance. It grows well in containers, allowing gardeners in cold winter areas (who must overwinter it indoors) to use it on a shady deck or patio. In warm winter areas, left to sprawl, it will become a groundcover. The light airy leaves are almost fern-like and the blooms are thick clusters of small white trumpets with pink outsides.

Growing Guide

Shade 1 to 2. Prune after blooming to keep the vine from tangling. Provide support or let it drift to become a groundcover. Grow jasmine in a container next to patio seating to be washed in fragrance. Keep plants watered regularly.

Kalmia latifolia.

Species, Varieties, Cultivars and Hybrids

J. polyanthum. An evergreen vine growing to 20 feet with lacy foliage and a spring explosion of very fragrant small trumpet blossoms pink on the outside and white inside. Zones 9 to 10.

Kalmia
Mountain laurel

A large 8- to 10-foot shrub with leathery leaves crowned with pink flowers in late spring. Other hybrid varieties come in colors from rose to red.

Growing Guide

Shade 1 to 3. Grow like rhododendrons.

Species, Varieties, Cultivars and Hybrids

K. latifolia 'Elf'. Dwarf form. Zones 5 to 9.

Mountain laurel flowers come in a variety of colors from red to pink to white.

The iris has long been a favorite perennial flower.

L

Mesclun.

Lactuca
Mesclun, assorted salad greens

Farmers in France have always offered their customers mixes of salad greens, called mesclun, for a variety of fresh flavors in a salad. Now you can buy pre-mixed mesclun seeds sold in one packet. There are mixes designed for early spring and fall, and those for the hotter summer months. All will grow successfully in light shade or in a location which only receives an hour or two of direct sun a day. Containers conveniently placed next to the kitchen can overflow with these easily grown greens.

Growing Guide

Shade 1 to 3. Sow the seeds thickly after the last chance of frost has passed in a container or directly in the ground according to the directions on the packet. Keep the soil moist until you see growth emerging. Watch out for slugs, snails and birds, who will also want to share the harvest. Harvest the greens by thinning the small lettuces when the leaves are only 2 inches long or use the cut-and-come-again method.

Species, Varieties, Cultivars and Hybrids

Mesclun mixes. (Check "Sources" list.)

Spring mixes may include flowering kale, mache, spinach, garden kale and early lettuces.

Summer mixes may include purslane, lettuces and arugula.

Lamium
Lamium

This perennial has burgundy-pink flushed leaves with a stripe down the middle. The small flowers are pink or white. Lamium makes a good 6-inch groundcover in shady areas under trees. A good plant for naturalizing.

Growing Guide

Shade 1 to 3. Plant in shady areas with moist, rich soil. The vine-like branches spread out 2 to 3 feet wide and up to 6

A variety of lettuces add an edible element to this shade garden.

The white-flowering form of lamium shows up well in heavily shaded areas.

Leptospermum
Australian tea tree

Seen either as a tall shrub with multiple trunks or a small and well-behaved tree, the Australian tea tree withstands drought, making it a star in the dry shade garden. As it prefers acid soil, it makes a good backdrop to acid-loving plants, as long as they like dry summer conditions. The white flowers in spring almost cover the tree. The small, grayish needle-like leaves make this a dainty specimen for the shade garden.

Growing Guide

Shade 1. Although most books specify full sun, it does well with just 2 to 3 hours of direct sun a day.

Species, Varieties, Cultivars and Hybrids

L. laevigatum, Australian tea tree. Grows to 30 feet high but can be pruned as a dense hedge. Although it likes sun, the tea tree tolerates shade, and its delicate size makes it useful in the

small shade garden. Tiny white flowers bloom in the spring. Zones 9 to 10.

Leucojum
Meadow snowflake, summer snowflake

Often confused with *Galanthus*, *Leucojum* sends up cheerful white bells one flower to a single stalk to bloom in early spring. Taller and blooming later than snowdrops, they naturalize well particularly in warm winter gardens. Plant a small number of bulbs and watch them spread. Hardy bulbs, they stand frost without complaint. Grows to 3 feet.

Growing Guide

Shade 1 to 2. Plant the bulbs in the fall 6 inches deep and spaced 3 inches apart. Make sure to keep the soil moist.

Species, Varieties, Cultivars and Hybrids

L. aestivum 'Gravetye Giant' is a handsome variety growing up to 3 feet tall. Zones 4 to 9.

Both lamium flowers and foliage are attractive.

inches tall. Grow in hanging baskets or plant as a ground-cover.

Species, Varieties, Cultivars and Hybrids

L. maculatum 'Beacon Silver'. Leaves look sprayed with silver paint. Zones 4 to 8.

L. m. 'Pink Pewter' has pink flowers and silvery-white leaves edged with green. Zones 4 to 8.

Lamium maculatum *'Aureum'* has golden foliage.

Summer snowflake.

Oriental lilies are some of the most spectacular lilies.

Lilium
Lily

One of the oldest cultivated flowers. Every shade garden should include lilies, for they are as hardy as daffodils and reliable as long as they are not deprived of water even when in dormancy. Some types grow quite tall with a strong perfume, so surrounding a shaded seating area with a thicket of lilies can provide a true aromatherapy experience.

Growing Guide

Unlike many bulbs that don't need water during their dormancy, lilies always want

moisture as they actually never stop growing (except in winter), even if they are not showing any foliage. Lilies want cool roots, so mulch thickly.

Species, Varieties, Cultivars and Hybrids

L. martagon, European lily. One of the best lilies for the shade, the 3- to 6-foot stems bear 12 or more flowers. Make sure to keep roots damp and cool with mulching and consistent moisture. Zones 4 to 8.

L. regale, regal lily. Superbly fragrant with tall stems bearing white flowers. Afternoon shade. Zones 4 to 8.

L. superbum, Turk's cap. A native plant with tall stems and orange blossoms, you may have a problem locating this reliable plant (see "Sources"). Zones 4 to 9.

Oriental hybrid 'Casablanca'. Must have afternoon shade for its fragrant white flowers. Protect in Zone 4, Zones 5 to 9.

Liriope
Lilyturf

Looking like a tufted grass, liriope is a tough, spreading

Lily 'Orange Mountain'.

groundcover attractive in borders or naturalized in woodland gardens. Only about 8 inches high, it is well behaved, especially in a Japanese-style garden clumped around rocks or large steppingstones. The white or lavender flowers in spike-like clusters are a big plus both in the garden and indoors as long-lasting cut flowers.

Growing Guide

Shade 1 to 2. Set in plants in early spring. Prune back old foliage in early spring before the new growth starts. You can divide up plants in the spring. Lilyturf grows well in containers. Blooms in late summer or fall.

Species, Varieties, Cultivars and Hybrids

L. muscari 'Big Blue'. An evergreen perennial growing with grass-like leaves to 12 inches tall with dark purple-blue flower stalks in the fall. Zones 6 to 10.

L. spicata, creeping lilyturf. An evergreen perennial growing with grass-like leaves to 12 inches and spreading up to 16 inches wide. Light lavender flowers in late summer. Zones 5 to 10.

Lobelia
Lobelia

Common in nurseries in the form of six-pack starters, lobelia tolerates shade and produces brilliant flowers in small spreading mounds about 8 inches high. In mild-winter climates,

Oriental lily 'Casablanca'.

Lobularia maritima.

Lilyturf has a lush, calming effect in the garden.

treat lobelia as a perennial. An excellent plant to fill in around new perennials or disguise the edge of a bog garden. Added to hanging begonias, lobelia makes a filmy froth that softens the look of the large leaves.

Growing Guide
Shade 1 to 2. Plant starts in the early spring. Water regularly.

Species, Varieties, Cultivars and Hybrids
L. erinus 'Crystal Palace'. Bronzy leaves with bright blue flowers usually an edging plant.

L. e. 'Cambridge Blue'. Green leaves with blue flowers on a compact growing plant that spreads only 4 to 6 inches wide.

L. e. 'Blue Cascade'. A spreading type suitable to pour over the sides of containers. Effective teamed with pendulous tuberous begonias.

Lobularia
Sweet alyssum
The honey fragrance of alyssum evokes memories of warm summer days. Alyssum is treated in cold winter areas as an annual. Usually set out as starts, alyssum reseeds itself freely. Fluffy clouds of white or purple bloom in light shade areas or as edging along walks or around seating areas. Grows quickly and blooms all summer long.

Growing Guide
Shade 1 to 2. Sow from seed and have bloom within six weeks. Set out starts early in spring. Shear the tops a month after blooming for repeat blooms.

Species, Varieties, Cultivars and Hybrids
L. maritima 'Carpet of Snow'. Compact white flowering type

growing up to 4 inches high and spreading in a circle 6 inches wide.

L. 'Rosie O'Day'. A pink-flowered type with a compact growth habit.

L. 'Oriental Night'. The blooms are deep violet with the plant mounding only up to 4 inches high.

Annual lobelia trails gracefully.

Liriope is great in the ground and in containers.

Lonicera

Honeysuckle

Most gardeners are familiar with the golden-yellow, trumpet-shaped blossoms we used to pluck to suck out the sweet drop of nectar at the end, as its common name describes. Other honeysuckle varieties grow well with less light, bringing their rampant growth and bright blooms into the shade garden. There are evergreen, deciduous, hardy and tender honeysuckle varieties.

Growing Guide

Shade 1 to 3. Plant where there is support for the climbing vine or use as a groundcover. Lonicera may not bloom in Shade 3.

Species, Varieties, Cultivars and Hybrids

L. x *americana*. A pink-flowering, deciduous, twining climber.

Fragrant yellow flowers tinged pink, appear in summer. Height to 23 feet. Zones 6 to 9.

L. japonica 'Halliana'. Evergreen twining climber with fragrant white flowers. Height to 30 feet. Zones 4 to 10.

Lunaria

Honesty, silver dollar plant

A fast-growing biennial which, left to its own devices, naturalizes. In spring, tall stalks of 24- to 30-inch plants light up shady areas with small pink flowers. In summer, the flowers become quarter-sized seed pods which, when the husks fall off, look silvery and translucent.

Lonicera heckrottii.

Use this plant as a low maintenance groundcover.

Growing Guide

Shade 1 to 3. Sow seeds in the spring after the last chance of frost; in mild winter areas, sow them in the fall. Make sure to locate them where they will not become a pest if they reseed.

Species, Varieties, Cultivars and Hybrids

L. annua 'Variegata'. White-and-green variegated leaves.

Lycopersicon

Tomato

Although you won't be able to grow huge beefsteak tomatoes in a shady garden, you can produce a tasty crop of cherry tomatoes and even early season varieties with some measure of success. Try cherry tomatoes in a large hanging basket, look for bush types called "determinate" to grow in containers, or plant the vine types, called "indeterminate." Both types of tomatoes need to be staked, so make sure to provide support for them when planting.

Growing Guide

Shade 1. Choose varieties that ripen quickly, called "early season" varieties. Start the seeds indoors 6 weeks before the last frost, or plant transplants directly in the ground when the soil has

Lonicera sempervirens.

Lunaria is often used in dried-flower arrangements.

varieties are bred to produce fruit with minimum temperatures. Although it may not be quite as sweet as fruit ripened with more sun, it will be distinctly more flavorful than ordinary grocery store varieties.

Lycoris
Magic lily, hardy amaryllis

Like amaryllis in appearance, *Lycoris* can stand up to cooler winter weather better than other members of the family. The blooms appear like magic in August after their summer dormancy, rising up on 3-foot stalks. The strap-like leaves burst out rather untidily after the blooms and continue through to the following summer. Provide consistent water to plants while they are in foliage.

Growing Guide

Shade 1 to 2. Plant as a summer bulb. When the blooms appear, begin to feed until leaves are fully mature. Plant 6 inches deep in a protected spot, such as under shrubs and trees or along a wall. Mulch heavily before the first frost.

Species, Varieties, Cultivars and Hybrids

L. squamigera. Late summer blooming with fragrant pink blossoms. Zones 6 to 10.

warmed. Make sure they receive at least 2 hours of direct sunlight a day. Train them up a trellis or stake them. Try growing the cherry types in a hanging basket or the bush types in a large container. Fertilize with a low-nitrogen mixture monthly and mulch well. Mix two or three types together for a beautiful display on the vine and on the platter.

Species, Varieties, Cultivars and Hybrids

Cherry tomatoes such as 'Sweet 100', 'Yellow Pear', 'Green Grape' or 'Sun Gold' are some of the best. Small fruits up to $1^1/2$ inches in width mature quickly on rampantly growing vines. Prolific, even with only a minimum of 2 to 4 hours of sun a day. Very early season varieties such as 'Stupice', 'Early Girl', 'Dona' or 'Early Boy' produce fruit at least 2 inches in width with a minimum of 2 to 4 hours of sun a day. The early

Lycoris blooms in late summer.

EDIBLES AND HERBS

Although you may think that shade prohibits raising any edibles for the table, you will find that you can serve up a variety of fine fruits and vegetables with a limited amount of direct sun. Experiment with varieties described as "early spring" and "fall" or "cool season" crops, growing them in the shade during the summer months. Try planting cherry tomatoes where they get only 2 hours of direct sun a day and you will find yourself gathering a crop of delectable summer fruit. Although many herbs prefer to be saturated with sunlight, there are others that grow luxuriantly in the shade.

M-N

Mahonias add to the shade garden with their divided, glossy leaves.

Species, Varieties, Cultivars and Hybrids

M. lomariifolia. An 8- to 10-foot-tall shrub with stiff, holly-like leaves. Should have afternoon sun. Yellow blooms in winter are followed by purple berries. Zones 8 to 10.

Maianthemum
Canada mayflower

Canada mayflower looks remarkably like hosta, but their blooms are small sprays of white blossoms on a stem that rises up from the leaves in late spring or early summer. Their rhizomes spread easily underground, forming an attractive groundcover of 4-inch-tall leaves. A fine groundcover for the woodland garden. If conditions are perfect, mayflower can become invasive.

Growing Guide

Shade 2 to 3. Plant out in moist, rich soil. Keep soil consistently moist. Use under shrubs or as drifts in woodland settings.

Species, Varieties, Cultivars and Hybrids

M. canadense, Canada mayflower. A low groundcover with two glossy green leaves. Spring flowers are followed by red berries. Zones 4 to 8.

Mahonia
Mahonia

An evergreen shrub to 10 feet tall. The unusual branches with leaves similar to holly give this plant the appearance of a large fern. Yellow flowers are borne profusely at the branch tips in autumn, winter or early spring followed by red fruit which brings birds into the garden. It must have afternoon shade to keep the leaves a bright, glossy green.

Growing Guide

Shade 1 to 3. Plant in a location where mahonia receives some shade. Give the plant plenty of room as it will grow quite tall.

Malus
Crabapple

One of the most useful of all the small, shade-happy trees, crabapples have it all: glorious flowers, edible fruit and fall display. Large fruiting types produce tart apples for jellies and pickles, but some varieties bear fruits smaller than a thimble to be enjoyed only by birds. Use the trees to line walkways, singly as a focal point in woodland gardens or as a fine patio tree. One or two trees can be a center of interest in a Japanese garden. Trees come in different sizes, from 10 feet to 30 feet depending upon variety and cultivar.

Growing Guide

Shade 1 to 2. Choose from over 200 varieties to find the one that best suits the garden, the needs of the gardener and the climate. Consider size, fruit, disease resistance and leaf color when making your decision.

Species, Varieties, Cultivars and Hybrids

Many different types, some with quite large and tasty crabapples, others suitable only for pickling and some inedible types.

Ostrich fern.

M. floribunda, Japanese flowering crabapple. Growing 15 to 25 feet, the Japanese flowering crabapple produces an extraordinarily prolific amount of blooms with a sweet fragrance. The small yellow fruit is inedible.

M. 'Transcendent'. One of the most popular for making preserves and jelly.

Matteuccia
Ostrich fern

One of the tallest ferns, growing up to 6 feet, the ostrich fern looks magnificent at the back of shade borders. The unfurling new fronds, called fiddleheads, are considered edible, but be cautious as not everyone can tolerate them. Given the right conditions, ostrich ferns will spread.

Growing Guide

Shade 1 to 3. Plant these ferns in rich, moist soil. Keep well watered throughout the summer. Prune off dead fronds.

Species, Varieties, Cultivars and Hybrids

M. pennsylvanica. Native to the East Coast, the ostrich fern can reach 6 feet tall and will

Lemon balm is one of the herbs that grows successfully in shade.

spread by underground rhizomes. Goes dormant in the winter. Zones 2 to 8.

M. struthiopteris. Grown on the West Coast and smaller than the East Coast variety only reaching about 3 feet tall. Zones 2 to 8.

Melissa
Lemon balm, sweet balm

Although it grows like a mint, lemon balm has lemon-scented leaves and is wonderful for making teas. Although not as strong as lemon verbena, lemon balm can be added to marinades for meats or simmered in a mixture of sugar and water to make a poaching liquid for fresh fruits. Well-mannered and not as invasive as mint, use lemon balm as a tall groundcover underneath pruned shrubs and canopy trees. Lemon balm tolerates drought so you can grow it in dry shade gardens.

Growing Guide

Shade 1 to 2. Plant transplants in a soil that drains well. If you use it in a dry garden, soak thoroughly when it looks wilted.

Species, Varieties, Cultivars and Hybrids

M. officinalis var. *variegata*, variegated lemon balm. The chartreuse-yellow and green leaves light up a shade border.

Malus floribunda.

Mentha
Mint

Mints come in all flavors, from spearmint to orange—even chocolate! Useful for sauces and soothing herbal teas, the chopped leaves also add spice to potato salad or fresh spring peas. Mints grow well in the shade, but they can be irritatingly invasive. They spread through their roots, sprouting up just weeks after you thought you had gotten the best of them. Still, fresh mint in iced tea makes it worthwhile to grow. But confine mint in containers or in a location where it can spread to become a groundcover but not a pest. Variegated mints make a wonderful accent, as does the neat and crisp appearance of the dark green spearmint.

Growing Guide

Shade 1 to 3. Set out plants in early spring or midsummer in a light shade area. Choose an area where you don't mind mint spreading. Or control the roots' spread by sinking plants grown in pots down into the ground. You can also grow mint in a container above ground. Mints will withstand some drought, but water consistently for the best appearance.

Species, Varieties, Cultivars and Hybrids

M. x *gentilis* 'Variegata', ginger mint. The plants have golden flecks and grow to more than 12 inches. Zones 4 to 9.

M. suaveolens 'Variegata', variegated applemint. The leaves have rounded edges, and plants grow to 3 feet. Zones 4 to 9.

Mertensia
Virginia bluebells

A useful perennial for the woodland garden, Virginia bluebells are 2-foot-tall plants that send up a bloom stalk covered in blue, funnel-shaped flowers in early spring. Like bleeding hearts, the plants die down soon after bloom, so mark the spots so you don't injure the clumps while they are dormant.

Growing Guide

Shade 2 to 3. Use bluebells at the back of a tall shady border or in a woodland garden paired with ferns and spring daffodils. Provide rich soil and keep it consistently moist. Mark the location of the clumps as the plants become dormant soon after spring bloom. Use summer-blooming annuals to cover the gaps they leave after they die down. Clumps left undisturbed will gradually spread. Protect the clumps from slug damage.

Species, Varieties, Cultivars and Hybrids

M. virginica, Virginia bluebells. A 2-foot-tall perennial with sprays of blue, funnel-shaped blooms in spring. A summer-dormant plant. Zones 4 to 9.

Microlepia

These drought-resistant ferns suit the dry shade garden. As tough as they are, however, they will only survive in a mild winter climate. Some are evergreen, some deciduous. Best in hanging baskets.

Growing Guide

Shade 1 to 3. These ferns want to dry out in between waterings. Grow them in hanging baskets or containers

Curly spearmint has an added bonus—crimped foliage.

where summer rains keep soil moist.

Species, Varieties, Cultivars and Hybrids

M. strigosa, lace fern. A finely cut evergreen fern that is sturdier than the delicate fronds indicate. Grows 2 to 3 feet tall. Zone 10.

Mimulus
Monkeyflower

Another flower, like the pansy, whose bloom seems to resemble a grinning monkey. Features a funnel-shaped flower that has two "lips" at the bottom. Whether or not you see the resemblance, you will enjoy this shade garden plant. Although it is a perennial, it is grown as an annual from seed or set out in the early spring as young starts.

Growing Guide

Seed monkeyflower in shady patches in early spring or set out young plants. Keep the soil moist. Use in borders, woodlands or plant in containers or hanging baskets.

Species, Varieties, Cultivars and Hybrids

M. hybridus, monkeyflower. A handsome 1¹/₂-foot-tall plant with multicolored flowers over the summer season with white-edged petals. Zones 6 to 9.

Muscari
Grape hyacinth

These little bulbs send up grassy leaves followed in the early spring by a stem with blue flowers that resemble closed grapes until they flare open at the tips. Look for white-flowered varieties and new types with the flowers each frilled at the bottom. Fully to half-hardy.

Growing Guide

Plant the bulbs in the fall in a woodland setting or as a spring border to a bulb garden. Let the bulbs become crowded in the ground or in containers.

Species, Varieties, Cultivars and Hybrids

M. armeniacum. A common variety that is very reliable. Zones 4 to 9.

M. botryoides. Most often sold. Look for hybridized cultivars in white or pink, frilled or plumed types. Zones 2 to 8.

Forget-me-nots are blue, white or pink.

Myosotis
Forget-me-not

These old-fashioned plants look good growing under shrubs or in a woodland setting. They flower in bright blue or white from late spring to summer. Left alone, they naturalize throughout a woodland.

Growing Guide

Shade 1 to 3. Forget-me-nots are hardy plants that want only to have water and light shade. Sow the seed in autumn or plant in early spring.

Species, Varieties, Cultivars and Hybrids

M. sylvatica 'Blue Ball'. A compact, slow-growing perennial that blooms in spring and early summer with spikes of tiny, deep-blue flowers. Grows up to 8 inches tall. Zones 5 to 8.

M. s. 'Victoria Alba'. A white-blooming variety up to 10 inches tall.

Forget-me-nots self-seed in many gardens and increase in number.

Grape hyacinth blooms profusely in the spring.

Daffodils bloom in the sun, before trees leaf out, and go dormant when it gets shady.

Narcissus
Daffodil

Daffodils are beloved symbols of the spring garden. Although they tolerate some shade, they bloom better with some sun and will carpet areas under deciduous trees year after year, popping out in bloom before the

Some varieties of daffodil naturalize easily.

trees leaf out. Still, some daffodils and *narcissus* stand shade, particularly if it is Shade 1, or in an area that receives direct morning or afternoon sun. Plant different varieties so you have a succession of blooms from early spring to summer. Protect the blossoms of early types from frost by planting in containers and protecting under a roof.

Growing Guide

Shade 1. Plant the bulbs in the fall, three times as deep as the circumference of the bulb. For a natural look in a woodland forest, plant in clumps of five or more bulbs, but make sure the bulbs don't touch and there is space for new bulblets to grow.

Scatter all-purpose, time-release fertilizer pellets over the area in the spring. Divide the clumps when blooms seem to diminish. Most hardy Zones 4 to 8.

Species, Varieties, Cultivars and Hybrids

Narcissus are categorized in divisions indicating the kind of blossom. For example, 'King Alfred', the classic yellow-trumpet daffodil, is in Division 1. Consider the following important divisions:

Division 1. Single-trumpet flowers—spring-flowering.

Division 2. Large cupped flowers—spring-flowering.

Division 5. Triandus: narrow reflexed petal—spring-flowering.

Division 7. Jonquil: fragrant flowers borne 2 to a stem—spring-flowering.

Division 8. Tanzetta: often fragrant with clusters of flowers—late autumn to mid-spring.

Nepeta
Catmint, catnip

With its whorls of purple blooms and light green leaves, catnip is a charming plant that makes an attractive addition to any garden. Unfortunately, cats find it equally attractive and will

Narcissus.

Moths and bees, as well as cats, are fond of catnip and catmint.

smash its shape by rubbing directly on it. In ancient Rome, it was used as a kitchen seasoning and medicine. To solve the cat problem, look for the form least attractive to felines, namely *N. mussinii*; a lower growing type with lots of lavender-blue flowers over a long blooming season.

Growing Guide

Shade 1 to 2. Set plants into a light shade location. Catnip can take some summer dryness but water consistently to maintain

best appearance. Catmint makes an excellent edging plant, perfect for the front of any mixed border planting.

Species, Varieties, Cultivars and Hybrids

N. cataria, catnip. The plant cats love, growing up to 3 feet high. Lavender or white flowers grow at the branch tips in the late spring. Zones 4 to 8.

N. x *faassenii* often sold as *N. mussinii*, a lower, more compact form less attractive to cats. Grows to 2 feet tall and as wide. Soft grayish foliage with spikes of purple flowers. Zones 4 to 8.

N. siberica, catmint. Grayish-blue foliage and lavender or blue flowers on 3-foot plants. Zones 4 to 8.

Nicotiana
Flowering tobacco

These plants are valued for their elegant upright shape and extremely fragrant flowers. However, the flowers exhibit their fragrance only at night, luring their pollinator—the night-flying hawk moth. Place the plants where you might sit out to view the moon or to relax after dinner so you can inhale the sweet night fragrance.

Growing Guide

Shade 1. The tiny seeds seem more like dust, so care is necessary when seeding, and it is advisable to start seeds in a container and then transplant. Plant in light shade or where the plants receive 2 to 4 hours of direct sun.

Species, Varieties, Cultivars and Hybrids

N. alata 'Grandiflora' has the strongest fragrance. Improved varieties may have no fragrance at all.

Catmint is a popular plant in many perennial gardens.

Flowering tobacco flowers in shades of red, pink, white and even green.

P

Pachysandra
Pachysandra, Japanese spurge

Pachysandra requires a shady situation with an acid soil, making it a good pairing with natural plantings of rhododendrons and azaleas. Because pachysandra grows in shade, it makes a good groundcover under trees and shrubs. The plant grows in clumps 8 to 12 inches high. Although there are small white flowers, they are insignificant. Use pachysandra in woodland gardens for a uniform appearance. Interplant with spring-blooming bulbs because pachysandra hides the yellowing foliage after the bulbs bloom.

Variegated pachysandra adds zing as a groundcover.

Peonies are some of the oldest of the old-fashioned flowers.

Growing Guide

Shade 2 to 4. Plant in rich, moist soil. Shear only if necessary. When using as a groundcover, set plants 6 inches apart to have a quick covering. Keep soil consistently moist while the plants become established. Applying a mulch just after planting ensures good results.

Species, Varieties, Cultivars and Hybrids

P. terminalis 'Variegata'. A variegated leaf form in green and white. Zones 5 to 8.

P. t. 'Green Carpet'. A compact form growing only 6 to 8 inches high.

Paeonia
Peony

Peonies are much beloved garden plants with huge fragrant

blooms of tender pinks and whites. There are two main kinds, tree and herbaceous peonies. The tree peonies produce flowers from the woody stems while the herbaceous peonies die back to the ground every year. As cut flowers, there is nothing more elegant than a single peony in a glass vase perfuming a whole room. Their elegant foliage looks good in a shady border all year long.

Growing Guide

Work sufficient quantities of organic material into the site before you plant peonies as they are long-lived perennials and do not want to be disturbed. Plant herbaceous peonies in the fall, or in the spring as bare-root plants. The tree peonies can be set in similarly in the fall or very early spring. Make sure to provide fertilizer after bloom and in the fall. Mulch and water consistently. Provide wire hoops or supports for the heavy flower heads.

Species, Varieties, Cultivars and Hybrids

P. lactiflora, herbaceous peonies. These cold-weather-

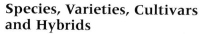

Pachysandra terminalis.

The native Virginia creeper has wonderful autumn foliage.

receive the first blooms. Zones 5 to 8.

Parthenocissus
Boston ivy

Woody-stemmed, deciduous vines climb with sucker-footed tendrils tenaciously attaching themselves to almost any vertical surface. In addition to its spring and summer leafy-greenness, *Parthenocissus* is also grown for the intense fall leaf colors that light up any fence or house wall.

Growing Guide

Shade 1 to 2. Give these vines plenty of room, for they will grow up to 50 feet long. Wonderful for covering anything. Be advised, however: Do not grow on any surface you may want to repaint.

Species, Varieties, Cultivars and Hybrids

P. quinquefolia, Virginia creeper. A vine with five-lobed leaves that grows up to 50 feet. Zones 4 to 9.

P. tricuspidata, Boston ivy. A vine with three-lobed leaves that grows to 70 feet. Zones 4 to 9.

Perilla
Chinese basil, shiso

The leaves' deep purple color makes them a hit in a mixed shade border. The leaves are edible, tasting a bit like cinnamon and a bit like mint. The Japanese fry the bloom stalks in a tempura batter. Easy to grow, perilla will reseed and can be invasive. At 2 to 3 feet tall, it does well in the middle of a border.

Virginia creeper can completely engulf a structure—plan your supports well.

Growing Guide

Shade 1 to 2. Happy in mixed borders or in deserted areas, perilla once established does not need to be kept moist. If you do not want it to self sow, which it does freely, cut off flower heads before they mature to seeds.

Species, Varieties, Cultivars and Hybrids

P. frutescens, Chinese basil, shiso. A tall-growing plant that comes with green or purple foliage. The purple is particularly handsome. Zones 8 to 10.

loving plants may not flower if winters are warm. Growing 3 to 4 feet tall, they bear blossoms in late spring or early summer 4 to 6 inches in width. Zones 3 to 8.

P. suffruticosa, tree peonies. As deciduous shrubs, they grow slowly to 3 to 5 feet. They prefer less winter cold and need to be protected from high winds. The large blossoms—as big as 10 to 12 inches wide—are not produced until the shrubs become established and grow some; so the gardener must be patient to

Pink peonies and coral bells complement each other well.

*Boston ivy is often confused with English ivy (*Hedera helix*).*

Primula *x* polyantha.

bursting out in the spring and sending up bloom stalks with long pendulous blossoms in white. Arching stems can act as a groundcover when naturalized.

Growing Guide

Shade 1 to 3. Excellent plants for the woodland garden, Solomon's seal can grow as tall as 6 to 7 feet depending on variety. Keep soil consistently moist. Do not divide clumps, but peel off rhizomes from the clump's edges in the early spring.

Species, Varieties, Cultivars and Hybrids

P. biflorum, great Solomon's seal, up to 5 feet tall. Zones 4 to 9.

P. multiflorum. 3 feet tall, fully hardy, look for the cultivar 'Variegatum' with green-and-white striped leaves. Zones 4 to 9.

Polemonium
Jacob's-ladder

Like a fern that blossoms, the delicate, lacy leaves of Jacob's-ladder are topped with bell-shaped blooms. Flowers in lavender shades droop from blooming stems from early

spring to summer. The stems can reach 1 1/2 feet tall, so plant Jacob's-ladder in the middle of a shady border or in clumps in a woodland setting.

Growing Guide

Shade 1 to 2. Plant Jacob's-ladder in the fall or early spring with ferns, columbine and hostas for a fine display. Water consistently.

Species, Varieties, Cultivars and Hybrids

P. caeruleum, Jacob's-ladder. Standing 1 1/2 feet tall, this fern-like plant produces clusters of hanging, bell-shaped, light blue flowers. Zones 4 to 8.

Polygonatum
Solomon's seal

A favorite shade plant, some varieties are less hardy than others, so choose according to your climate. These graceful plants grow from rhizomes,

Polystichum

A group of very useful evergreen ferns that are somewhat drought tolerant. Once established they make great circles of fronds. Excellent in woodland gardens.

Growing Guide

Shade 1 to 2. Although mature plants need little water, keep soil moist until the ferns are established. They do best in a soil rich in humus. Mulch heavily. Prune

Solomon's seal has very divided leaves that look something like a ladder.

Solomon's seal is a native North American plant adapted to the shade.

Primroses have long been favorite flowers in England, but they grow well here too.

off the dead fronds to keep the ferns looking tidy.

Species, Varieties, Cultivars and Hybrids

P. acrostichoides, Christmas fern. An evergreen fern with dark green fronds 2 feet long. Zones 4 to 9.

P. munitum, Western sword fern. Leathery fronds can grow to be 2 to 4 feet long. Zones 6 to 9.

P. setiferum, soft shield fern. A large fern with filmy fronds 2 to 4¹/₂ feet tall that makes a good backdrop to begonias and impatiens. Zones 6 to 8.

Primula
Primrose

Flowering perennials and annuals that bring bright spring or summer bloom to the shade garden. There are enough varieties that collectors gather them from others to fill out their collections. Many perennials are used as annuals where the summers are hot and dry. The flowers rise on stalks above crinkly leaves in almost all ranges of colors. Primroses are a favorite accompaniment to daffodils and other spring bulbs.

Growing Guide

Shade 1 to 2. Grow primroses in part shade, with consistent moisture. Provide more shade

in areas where the summers are hot and dry. Use primroses as border edgings, in containers, around trees and in drifts under tall trees.

Species, Varieties, Cultivars and Hybrids

P. malacoides, fairy primrose. Evergreen with tall, white or pink tiny flowers on 8- to 15-inch stems.

P. polyantha, polyanthus primrose. Flower stems rise 8 to 10 inches tall above green crinkled leaves. The flowers start in early spring and continue until early summer and bloom in every imaginable color. Zones 5 to 8.

Prunus
Plum, cherry, almond

Growing fruit in shady gardens in not an impossible feat, and well worth the effort. Success depends upon picking the sunniest spot in the garden and matching it to an unfussy fruit variety. Growing against a south- or west-facing wall to increase heat aids in fruit production. Dwarf varieties take less space, particularly when pruned flat against a fence or along the back of a border. Check with local nurseries for varieties most successful in your climate. If trees need two

Most lungworts flower in shades of blue, pink or white.

Lungworts flower early in sping, but the spotted foliage of variegated types looks good all season.

varieties to cross-pollinate, plant two trees in one hole.

Pulmonaria
Lungwort

Although the flowers are pleasing, it is the lungwort's leaves that make it worth including in the shade garden. Wonderfully spotted—sometimes in silver, sometimes in pink—pulmonaria deserves a place in the shade garden for the variety it brings. Lungworts grow 6 to 12 inches tall.

Growing Guide

Shade 1 to 3. Grows happily in the company of rhododendrons and azaleas. Use as a ground cover or in the company of hostas and ferns.

Species, Varieties, Cultivars and Hybrids

P. longifolia. Silver-spotted thin leaves up to 20 inches long. Blooms later in spring than other types. Zones 4 to 8.

P. saccharata, Bethlehem sage. Silver-spotted leaves on stems that rise 1¹/₂ feet tall with blue, funnel-shaped flowers in spring. Zones 4 to 8.

R

Rhododendron

Rhododendrons and azaleas

One of the best groups of shade-loving shrubs, rhododendrons and azaleas come in hundreds of colors and sizes, truly one for any kind of situation or use. The botanical classification system lumps these two types of shrubs together although rhododendrons have a different flower structure and are evergreen or semi-evergreen, while azaleas can be evergreen or deciduous. Rhododendrons can become the size of small trees while azaleas stay a more modest height—up to 5 feet at maximum. Colors range from white to pinks, deep reds, purples, yellows and oranges. Blooms are rarely deeply fragrant, although *R.* x *fragrantissimum* is one of the rare types that can perfume a garden.

Growing Guide

Shade 1 to 2. Both azaleas and rhododendrons have similar growing preferences for filtered shade and moist, well-drained soil. They are shallow-rooted and like to be mulched—preferably with pine needles or oak leaves to encourage acid soil, with no cultivation in their root zones that might disturb the roots. Provide consistent water throughout the summer. Cut off old flower blooms when possible. Both rhododendrons and azaleas grow well in containers as long as provided with consistent water.

Species, Varieties, Cultivars and Hybrids

Rhododendrons: Look for the size and shape to fit your planting need. Rhododendrons range from hardy to half-hardy so choose the type according to your climate.

Azaleas: Can be evergreen or deciduous, and they are smaller with smaller leaves than the rhododendrons. Grown for their spring bloom, they provide a green screen the rest of the year.

Azalea.

Rosa

Rose

Roses are perfect companions to shade gardens—both in the many, many roses happy to clamber up fences, pergolas, arbors and patios to provide shade during hot summer months, as well as a smaller selection of roses which tolerate some shade. If you have a shady garden and want to include roses, choose the type carefully and make sure the planting site has at least 2 hours of direct morning or afternoon sun. For a splendid display, team roses with clematis, pruning both carefully after bloom to allow air circulation for both plants and prevent mildew and other fungal diseases.

Azaleas are great for brightening up many a shady spot.

Rhododendron 'Paprika Spice'.

Thanks to modern breeding, there are azaleas and rhododendrons for almost every part of the country.

Pink rhododendrons and redbuds are a perfect spring combination.

ease-resistant and hardy.

Rosmarinus
Rosemary

Rosemary is tolerant of shade conditions as long as it receives 2 or more hours of direct sun a day. Long used as a culinary herb, there are many forms of rosemary that can be used in a variety of ways in the garden: as a groundcover, a clipped hedge, a small standard topiary, a 6-foot-tall shrub or even as a container plant. Look for the unusual pink- or white-flowered varieties or the unusual variegated form, '*Variegatum*', with yellow and green leaves.

Growing Guide

Shade 1 to 2. Rosemary should be planted in early spring; in mild winter climates, plant in late summer. Once established, rosemary withstands summer drought. Make sure to choose the variety specific to the site where you plan to use it.

Species, Varieties, Cultivars and Hybrids

R. officinalis 'Variegatum'. Variegated leaves on a 4- to 6-foot-tall shrub. Zones 7 to 9.

Growing Guide

Shade 1 to 2 depending upon variety. Choose plants that fit the space available in the garden, for some climbers can grow to 20 feet or more. Protect roses against extreme winter cold by heavily mulching the roots. Prune according to the type of rose, for untimely pruning may shear off blossom wood. Feed and water regularly during the growing season.

Species, Varieties, Cultivars and Hybrids

R. 'Cecile Brunner'. Small pink flowers that are lightly fragrant erupt in spring. Makes a good vine to clamber through an open branched tree. Zones 5 to 9.

R. 'Sutters Gold'. Climbing hybrid tea rose with vigorous growth and lovely fragrance.

R. 'Allen Chandler'. One of Vita Sackville-West's favorites used to cover the brick entry of Sissinghurst Castle. A red semi-double with golden stamens that repeat blooms.

R. 'Madame de Carriere'. Noisette climbing rose with fragrant creamy just pink blossoms. Climbs 18 to 25 feet.

R. 'New Dawn'. One of the best for a north-facing wall, with repeating pink-tinged fragrant blooms. Will grow to 15 feet.

R. 'Iceberg'. In both climbing and non-climbing forms, dis-

R. o. 'Albus'. White flowers on a 4- to 6-foot tall shrub. Zones 7 to 9.

R. o. 'Majorca Pink'. Pink flowers on a 4- to 6-foot-tall shrub. Zones 7 to 9.

R. o. 'Tuscan Blue'. Grows with upright thrusting stems to 6 feet tall. Zones 7 to 9.

R. o. 'Prostratus' is 6 inches tall but not cold tolerant. Zones 7 to 9.

CLIMBING ROSE FAVORITES

There are hundreds and hundreds of climbing tea roses, polyanthas, floribundas and even climbing miniature roses. Check with your local nursery or regional botanical garden for the outstanding roses that suit your area.

Climbing roses are perfect for lightly shaded arbors or trellises.

S-T

Sagina
Irish moss

A quick-growing groundcover that tolerates shade and forms a low green mat. Tiny white flowers polka dot the green. Particularly effective as a lawn substitute or to substitute for moss in a Japanese-style garden. Useful to edge around paving stones.

Growing Guide

Shade 1 to 2. Set starts in rich, moist soil in early spring. Plant in the shade so the roots stay cool and moist, like the Irish climate.

For a moss-like effect, plant baby's tears in a shady spot.

Irish moss is another moss-like plant for the shade garden.

Species, Varieties, Cultivars and Hybrids

S. subulata, Irish moss. A low-growing groundcover that can be a lawn substitute. Will spread quickly if keep watered. Zones 5 to 9.

Sanguinaria
Bloodroot

A spreading perennial with underground rhizomes that, when cut, run with red sap (the basis for the common name). Growing to 4 to 6 inches tall, it spreads to foot-wide circles in rich, moist soil. In spring, bloodroot is covered with white, daisy-like flowers except for the petals. Bloodroot is a good choice for woodland gardens as a natural-looking groundcover, or in a rock garden.

Growing Guide

Plant in early spring in humus-rich soil kept consistently moist. Plants are summer dormant, so mark the spot when the plant dies down so you don't disturb the rhizomes during dormancy.

Species, Varieties, Cultivars and Hybrids

S. canadensis. A useful plant for the woodland garden covered with white flowers in the spring. The low-growing, 4- to 6-inch plant bears flowers singly on 8-inch stems. Zones 3 to 8.

Scilla (See also Endymion)

Scilla
Squill

Easy bulbs for the shade garden, their only requirements are for winter and early spring sun, making them perfectly suited for planting under deciduous trees. The flowers can be bell-shaped or spikes, often in shades of blue. Squirrels and other wood creatures may nibble on the blossoms.

Growing Guide

Shade 1 to 3 as long as they have winter sun. Plant out in the fall under deciduous trees, or where they can receive direct sun during the winter and early spring. In summer, they prefer shade. Only 3 to 6 inches high, plant them where they will not be obscured by taller plants.

Species, Varieties, Cultivars and Hybrids

S. siberica, Siberian squill. Bright blue flowers. Zones 4 to 8.

S. mischtschenkoana. White flowers with blue stripes stand out in shaded spots.

Sedum
Stonecrop

Sedums are succulents useful for the shade garden as they tolerate shifting sun patterns and are drought resistant. There are low, 2- to 3-inch-high types excellent for edging garden beds or growing in containers. Taller types can fill out borders. Some sedums have light, frosty green petals while others, such as pork and beans, have petals swollen to jelly-bean size in bright green and reddish tones. Their succulent petals store water, which is

what makes them so successful as drought-resistant plants. However, the amount of water stored in the petals makes them frost tender.

Growing Guide

Set out plants in well-worked soil. Use the smaller types in rock gardens, containers or as edging along garden beds. If using as a ground cover, set plants 10 to 12 inches apart. Water to establish plants, then water as needed.

Species, Varieties, Cultivars and Hybrids

S. acre 'Aureum', gold-moss sedum. A low-growing mat with yellow leaves 2 to 5 inches tall and covered with yellow blooms in spring. Hardy. Zones 4 to 9.

S. morganianum, donkey tail. A sedum with pendulous branches, excellent in hanging containers. Zone 10.

S. spectabile. A 1^{1}/$_{2}$-foot-tall sedum with showy pink flowers over late summer and autumn. An excellent plant for back of borders. Also called *Hylotelephium.* Zones 4 to 9.

Soleirolia
Baby's tears

This charming plant forms a dense groundcover of bright green with very tiny leaves; also known as mind-your-own-business or mother-of-thousands. The latter describes its aggressive

Baby's tears are great for covering ground between steppingstones.

growth pattern, which makes it an excellent spreading ground-cover in moist, shady places. Use it as a groundcover in lath houses or in a north-facing garden.

Growing Guide

Shade 1 to 3. Plant in shade where it receives a generous amount of moisture all year long. Feed generously once a year. Will freeze to a blackened mass after frosts, but generally returns from the roots.

Species, Varieties, Cultivars and Hybrids

S. soleirolii, baby's tears. A perennial with tiny leaves that in moist, humus-rich soil, will spread to make a dense, low— 1- to 2-inch—carpet. Zone 10.

S. s. 'Aurea'. A golden-green variety. Zone 10.

Highly contrasting coleus colors, such as red and green, are very showy.

Coleus come in a wide variety of colors—the lighter ones look best in shade.

Solenostemon
Coleus

Coleus, with their bright variegated leaves in shades of pink with green and white splashes, or deep Persian rug colors, enliven a shady area. Although they can be perennials in warm winter areas, most gardeners set them out as annuals. They contrast wonderfully when interplanted with impatiens.

Growing Guide

Shade 1 to 3. Plant early in spring and feed and water regularly. Pinch back the stems to encourage side growth to keep the plant looking handsome and bushy. Some gardeners pinch out bloom stalks to maintain shape. In the fall, before the first frost, take cuttings to root in water to overwinter, or dig up plants and keep them as houseplants.

Species, Varieties, Cultivars and Hybrids

C. 'Oriental Splendor' is a large-leafed variety.

C. 'Carefree' has ruffled leaves.

Styrax japonicus
Japanese snowbell

A deciduous tree that grows slowly to 30 feet in the garden. In early summer, great quantities of bell-shaped, fragrant flowers break out amongst the dark-green, glossy leaves. In the fall, the leaves turn from red to yellow.

Growing Guide

Shade 1 to 2. Plant in part shade, giving the tree plenty of water throughout the year. Prune to make sure it maintains its tree shape and to allow light in to planting beds underneath.

Species, Varieties, Cultivars and Hybrids

S. japonicum 'Pink Chimes'. A rare type with pink flowers that grows to 30 feet. Pink blooms in the spring and fall color make this small tree useful for maximum show. Zones 5 to 9.

Symphytum
Comfrey

Comfrey has spear-shaped, soft, furry leaves resembling foxglove. Like foxglove, it has long been used for medicinal purposes. In a sunny location it can be invasive, but in shade it is less aggressive. Small purple, tubular-shaped flowers hang down in a demure display from 3-foot-tall plants. Naturalize comfrey in a woodland garden, use it in shady borders or plant it as a carpet under tall shrubs where it looks like a natural planting.

Growing Guide

Shade 1 to 2. Set in plants or sow seeds in the spring in a light shade location. In mild winter areas it grows as a perennial; in cold winter areas grow it as a self-seeding annual.

Species, Varieties, Cultivars and Hybrids

S. grandiflorum. Pink or creamy white flowers.

S. officinale. A tall 2-foot plant with bell-shaped flowers in summer. There is a white-flowered

Red-leafed coleus cultivars are often particularly striking.

For a tropical look in the shade garden, consider using coleus.

Common comfrey.

Styrax japonicus.

Yews are highly ornamental shrubs that have many uses in the garden.

form as well as the purple. Zones 5 to 8.

S. o. 'Variegatum'. A pretty yellow-and-green variety.

Tanacetum parthenium, syn. *Chrysanthemum parthenium*

Feverfew

Although the books all say that feverfew takes full sun, this biennial grows successfully in filtered shade and is happy with next to no water. The leaves have a strong smell, reputed to ward off moths, while the roots have been used as a folk medicine to cure a variety of ills. In the garden, it is a useful filler, with almost fern-like, finely cut leaves and daisy blossoms.

Growing Guide

Shade 1 to 2. Sow seeds in fall or make divisions from clumps.

Will take summer drought. Unfussy. It reseeds readily.

Species, Varieties, Cultivars and Hybrids

C. parthenium 'Golden Ball' has yellow flowers.

C. parthenium 'Aureum' or 'Golden Feather' has lemon-green foliage. Wonderful to perk up a shady border.

Taxus

Yew

Evergreen conifers, yews make a good shade hedge, low or high. They are slow-growing and long-lived, and can be shorn or pruned.

Growing Guide

Shade 1 to 3. Plant yews in a well-drained soil in spring or autumn. Some have red, fleshy "berries" surrounding poisonous seeds.

Species, Varieties, Cultivars and Hybrids

T. baccata. A tree growing to 70 feet with many smaller cultivars. Some, such as 'Fastigiata Aurea' are variegated.

T. cuspidata, Japanese yew. Shrub or tree to 2 feet with many smaller cultivars. Zones 4 to 8.

Thymus

Thyme

Useful in light shade, some types of thyme make a ground-hugging, low mat of green. Others grow up to 7 to 8 inches and can be sheared for an infor-

mal hedge. There are also silver-and-green and yellow-and-green variegated types. Of course, thyme is celebrated as a culinary herb—added to breads or used in stews, casseroles and baked meats from chicken to veal. Thyme is included as part of the classic French seasoning *bouquet garni* (along with parsley and bay leaf) and is also one of the ingredients the monks use in making Benedictine, the well-known liquor from France.

Growing Guide

Shade 1. Set out plants in part shade in the early spring or midsummer.

Species, Varieties, Cultivars and Hybrids

T. x citriodorus 'Aureus'. Golden-yellow leaves with a citrus fragrance. Zones 6 to 8.

T. x c. 'Silver Queen'. Silvery-white foliage. Zones 6 to 8.

T. vulgaris, Common thyme. The culinary herb. Zones 6 to 9.

For use in cooking or as a groundcover, thyme has a place in the garden.

Feverfew.

Tiarella *is a native groundcover related to coral bells.*

Tiarella
Allegheny foamflower

A groundcover that spreads by runners with spikes of white flowers in late spring. The light green leaves turn bronze-red after the first frost. This groundcover won't be invasive for a woodland garden or at the front of a shady border as it grows only about 8 inches tall.

Growing Guide

Shade 1 to 3. Plant in early spring in moist, rich soil. Don't disturb it if you want it to spread.

Species, Varieties, Cultivars and Hybrids

T. cordifolia, Allegheny foam-flower. A low-growing ground-cover 6 to 8 inches tall. Spreads to 12 inches wide. In the spring, spikes of tiny, white blossoms look like filmy foam above the light green lobed leaves. Zones 4 to 9.

Trillium
Wake-robin

Called wake-robin to indicate its very early spring bloom, trilliums are characterized by the three leaves with the flower rising from the middle. Perfect as a groundcover for the woodland garden, they naturalize well with ferns. The neat appearance of trillium transfers just as well to a small garden with a shady border.

Growing Guide

Shade 2 to 3. A rhizome, trilliums prefer shade and moist, rich soil. Plant

the rhizome 3 to 4 inches deep in fall.

Species, Varieties, Cultivars and Hybrids

With their growing popularity, a wide variety of different types are becoming increasingly available. Some are hardy to Zone 3.

Tropaeolum
Nasturtium

These vining annuals can be treated as perennials in warm winter areas. If they have some summer moisture, nasturtiums can be used as a groundcover or as edging plants that creep into pathways. Nibble on their edible leaves or flowers, and pickle the seeds like capers. Use them in hanging baskets.

Growing Guide

Shade 1 to 2. Sow nasturtium seeds in early spring. Watch out for slugs and snails that feast on the new sprouts as well as the mature leaves. If you cover the bed with a mulch in the fall, the plants will self-sow from last year's seeds.

Species, Varieties, Cultivars and Hybrids

T. majus, garden nasturtium. There are both climbing types

Trilliums are beautiful, native flowers that thrive in the shade garden.

Tropaeolum majus *'Whirlibird'.*

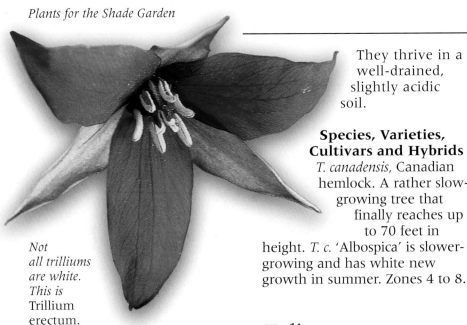

Not all trilliums are white. This is Trillium erectum.

Tulipa turkestanica.

They thrive in a well-drained, slightly acidic soil.

Species, Varieties, Cultivars and Hybrids

T. canadensis, Canadian hemlock. A rather slow-growing tree that finally reaches up to 70 feet in height. *T. c.* 'Albospica' is slower-growing and has white new growth in summer. Zones 4 to 8.

Tulipa
Tulip

The hybrid varieties are widely known, but less recognized are the species tulips which are smaller but no less showy in their own way. They naturalize in the shade garden, reappearing year after year in great drifts of color.

Growing Guide

Shade 1 to 2. These smaller-blossoming tulips get lost at the back of the border. Plant them out front where they can be seen. Plant bulbs in the fall.

Species, Varieties, Cultivars and Hybrids

T. tarda or *T. dasystemon*. 5 to 7 inches tall with white flowers and a yellow center. Zones 5 to 8.

T. turkestanica, Turkestan tulip. Zones 5 to 8.

which can become 6-foot vines for groundcover, or a compact type to 15 inches tall. 'Alaska' is a variegated leaf variety.

Tsuga
Hemlock

A graceful evergreen tree, the hemlock is one of the most beautiful conifers. It has something of a feathery appearance from a distance. Up close, it has glossy dark green needles with bands of white on the undersides and small cones.

Growing Guide

Shade 1 to 3. Hemlocks need a moist soil and protection from the sun in winter.

Trillium kurabayashii *has attractive foliage throughout the season.*

Tulipa tarda.

V-Z

Vinca *is a rapidly growing groundcover.*

*The var-
iegated
types of
vinca are
especially
showy in
shady
areas.*

Vaccinum
Blueberry

Blueberries grow in the same situation as rhododendrons and azaleas: rich humus soil with an acid balance that is moist all year long. They are valued as a hedge with fall color and handsome winter skeletons, as well as for their delicious fruit. You can grow blueberries in containers if you wish. The flowers in spring are small and bell-shaped and if you can keep people from eating the fruit, the blueberries look elegant when they ripen.

Growing Guide

Set in blueberries as bareroot plants or from a container. Make sure to work the soil so there are plenty of amendment-rich ingre-

Vinca *has pretty white or blue flowers.*

dients for the plants. Mulch well with oak leaves or pine needles to satisfy the plants' need for acid-balanced soil. Water consistently to keep soil moist.

Species, Varieties, Cultivars and Hybrids

V. angustifolium, lowbush blueberries. A low-growing type with sweet berries, useful as a woodland groundcover up to 2 feet tall.

V. corymbosum, highbush blueberries. The most common type of blueberry. Use the 6-foot shrubs as a hedge. Chose among the many different cultivars for early, midseason and late season berries for a succession of fruit throughout the summer.

Vinca
Periwinkle, myrtle

Periwinkle's cheerful, five-petaled, blue flowers seem vivid in the shade. The groundcover spreads effectively and will swallow anything smaller in its wake. Good for low-maintenance areas.

Growing Guide

Shade 1 to 3. Vinca can be left to naturalize in both wet and dry situations. Can be mowed periodically to neaten its appearance.

Viola x wittrockiana.

Species, Varieties, Cultivars and Hybrids

V. major. Long stems spread out, sometimes mounding to 2 feet. Zones 7 to 9.

V. minor, Dwarf periwinkle. A miniature form that is less drought resistant. Also variegated forms. Zones 4 to 8.

Viola

Viola, pansy

Although it seems inaccurate to lump all these together, they are all members of the same family and are invaluable to the

Violas look pretty and also have edible flowers great for garnishing desserts.

ANNUALS AND BIENNIALS

Annuals' intransigence gives them the advantage of being impermanent, so they provide seasonal bloom, fit in spaces in between newly planted perennials or fill containers for a color splash in a garden. Annuals can be started from seed, free sown or planted in place. Heirloom annuals are open pollinated—not hybrid types—and come true to the parent in succeeding years so they can be saved and replanted. Some annuals self-sow easily, making them great candidates for naturalizing.

Biennials linger a bit longer, growing from seed one season then blooming the next. Often gardeners start biennials from seed in the late summer or fall to allow at least 6 weeks before the first frost and set the timing so they bloom the following summer.

Both types play a part in the shade garden, particularly for those plants which self-sow. Instead of thinking of them as weeds, put them to work in out-of-the-way areas where you don't spend much time. The self-seeding types reward the gardener with plants and blooms without effort. Thank you indeed!

shade gardener. In mild winter areas, pansies and Johnny-jump-ups bloom all winter along. They can be used as border edgings, colorful groundcovers or in containers. Violets will mass to be a successful groundcover, especially under shrubs.

Growing Guide

Shade 1 to 2. Plant in light shaded areas. Particularly useful interplanted with bulbs to obscure dying foliage.

Species, Varieties, Cultivars and Hybrids

V. odorata, sweet violet. Feed in early spring, let young plants fill in empty spots.

The sunny yellow and purple flowers of some violas announce spring's arrival.

V. tricolor, Johnny-jump-up. Self-sows. Can be from 6 to 12 inches tall.

V. x wittrockiana, pansy. Plant out mixed colors or use all one shade.

Violas are a great choice to naturalize.

Viola canadensis.

Wisteria is one of the most popular flowering vines—it has pretty, fragrant flowers and pleasing foliage.

Wisteria

Wisteria

Wisteria's display of hanging clusters of purple or white flowers, sweetly fragrant in early spring, enhances any garden. But there are drawbacks to this gorgeous beauty. With its rampant growth, its stems become so heavy it can collapse all but the strongest arbors and pergolas. Wisteria can overwhelm a small garden with its intense growth, so the proper planting location is essential. This deciduous vine grows to 30 feet or more and is perfect for creating shade, covering arbors and running down long fences. It must have sun to bloom. Hardiness depends on variety, but some are fully hardy.

Growing Guide

Shade 1. Choose a sunny location, give it plenty of room to ramble, and build a *strong* structure for its support. As it grows, tie the vine to the support, as it has no tendrils but climbs by twining. Prune after flowering, and if necessary, prune again in late summer to thin woody stems.

Species, Varieties, Cultivars and Hybrids

W. floribunda, Japanese wisteria. 'Alba' is white. Flowers appear after leaves emerge in spring for a longer but less showy display. Zones 5 to 10.

Woodwardia fimbriata.

Tree ferns are perfect for adding a tropical accent to the shade garden.

Calla lilies are great shade garden plants, and the flowers are superb for cutting.

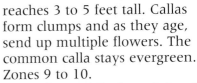

W. *fimbriata*, giant tree fern. Can be as large as 9 feet tall in moist woodland gardens, although usually it is only 4 to 5 feet tall. Sometimes sold as W. *chamissoi* or W. *radicans*. Zones 8 to 10.

Zantedeschia
Calla lily

A South African bulb that naturalizes in warm winter climates, particularly in boggy places. Stays green all winter long. It likes a wet growing season but can take a long, dry summer. There are smaller hybrids that do well in containers in colors of pinks and yellows.

Growing Guide

Shade 1. Plant the rhizomes 4 to 6 inches deep spaced 2 feet apart. Plant the hybrids in more acid soil under about 2 inches of soil. Plant them in containers, one to a 6-inch pot buried 2 inches under the potting mix. Water sparingly until foliage appears. In cold winter climates, let the bulbs go dry at the end of the summer, then lift and store with your other bulbs in a cool, dry place.

Species, Varieties, Cultivars and Hybrids

Z. *aethiopica*. The common calla with a white bloom reaches 3 to 5 feet tall. Callas form clumps and as they age, send up multiple flowers. The common calla stays evergreen. Zones 9 to 10.

Z. *rehmanni*. Red or pink calla on smaller stems. The plant dies down in late summer. Zones 9 to 10.

W. *sinensis*, Chinese wisteria. 'Alba' is white. Flowers burst out before leaves for a stunning display of blooms. Zones 5 to 9.

W. *venusta*, silky wisteria. 'Alba Plena' has double white flowers with a yellow blotch. Leaves carry silky hairs. Chunky clusters of bloom open all at once just as leaves are opening. Zones 5 to 10.

Woodwardia
Giant chain fern

One of the largest North American ferns, this plant can be found in shady spots from British Columbia to Mexico. Its bold silhouette makes it handsome against a wall or light-colored background. Plant behind lower-growing, more finely textured ferns.

Growing Guide

Shade 1 to 2. Keep the soil moist until the fern has become established.

Species, Varieties, Cultivars and Hybrids

W. *areolata*, netted tree fern. Fronds 1 to 2 feet long. Zones 5 to 9.

Zantedeschia aethiopica.

⟨ CHAPTER 6 ⟩
MAKING THE MOST OF SHADE

Gardeners could be called the original ecologists. Since the beginning of mankind (which coincides with the beginning of gardening), gardeners have been watching how wind, rain, water, soil, temperature and plants interact, and identifying which plants thrive and which decline. Nature is the teacher and we are the students. Shade gardening is no more difficult or easy than gardening in the sun. Yet though many of the same rules apply, the lack of light causes different effects and results.

In both the shade garden and the bright sun garden, the challenge of creating a fine garden is like weaving cloth: The interaction of color, texture and height are the strands to be woven together. Like pieces of art, each garden is completely different and completely personal. Sometimes we follow the rules, sometimes we break them: No matter what, we learn from what happens by observing our plants and really looking at the garden. With experience and experimentation, trying different combinations and learning new techniques, we get better and better at what we do.

GETTING TO KNOW THE RHYTHM OF YOUR GARDEN

Calanthea leaves are just one of hundreds of variegated plants available. Place green and white variegated plants in clumps down a border to lead the eye, or use for dramatic effect as a focal point.

Photosynthesis

Epidermal cells
Palisade cells
Mesophyll cells
Epidermal cells
Stomata
sunlight
oxygen
carbon dioxide
Stomata
oxygen
carbon dioxide
water

Leaves breathe through their pores, inhaling carbon dioxide and exhaling oxygen and water vapor. Using the energy of the sunlight acting on the chlorophyll in its cells, the plant manufactures the sugars that promote growth. The process of transforming light into food is called photosynthesis, while the circulation of water and oxygen drawn up from the roots through the stem of the plant and onto the surface of the leaves is called transpiration.

the lengthening of the days as the warmth of summer brings out the growth in our plants, and then the return to shorter days that signal the end of the growing season. With that comes the gradual hardening of summer's growth in preparation for the cold days of winter. As spring blossoms fade to summer's harvest, we prepare for the eventual coloring of the leaves and then the bare skeleton of winter's trees and shrubs. We observe nature's patterns and so become part of the natural process again.

Understanding the Mechanism of Plant Growth

The first step to becoming a better gardener is simply understanding how a plants works. Plants, like people, have requirements which must be met for them to grow. Understanding the basics of plant chemistry assists the gardener in meeting their plants' needs. As gardeners, our job is to provide the best environment for the plants to grow within their prescribed existence. Shade plants in particular need extra care because their special environment makes them live a

Regardless of our skill, a garden must grow at its own pace, must have a number of seasons to mature, and must meld together to look like "whole cloth." Gardens teach us patience, that there are things that cannot be rushed. For instance, a tree will grow only at its own speed. In this modern day, when we can order so many aspects of our lives and insulate ourselves against hot or cold inside snug houses, gardens remind us of the simple rhythms of nature. Watch

Large leaves allow a shade-loving plant to absorb more light so it can survive lower light levels than most plants.

Hosta's thin leaves betray its thirsty ways. The plant cannot store much water in its leaves so it needs a constant supply to its roots in order to sustain itself.

The thin, tender leaves of the bird's nest fern (Asplenium nidus) *will burn if exposed to direct sunlight.*

bit more on-the-edge than plants luxuriating in full light.

Although we have figured out the mysteries of traveling through space we do not yet thoroughly understand the process of photosynthesis, the way a plant absorbs light and translates it into energy that fuels growth. Remember, though, that light is not the same thing as direct sunlight. Plants survive in the shade on reflected light.

A plant absorbs light through its leaf surfaces, and draws in carbon dioxide through its leaf pores. The roots absorb water and nutrients from the soil which the plant translates into sugars in the complex chemical process know as photosynthesis. Using the energy from the light, the chlorophyll in the leaves of the plant chemically changes the water and carbon dioxide it draws in through the leaf to fuel for its growth. (See photosynthesis sidebar.)

Plants that grow in the shade have more chlorophyll in their leaves to convert the low levels of light into the energy that fuels their growth. You can often tell a shade plant from its leaves. Many shade-loving plants have large thin leaves, the better to draw in more light for their survival. Should sun come pouring in suddenly—for instance if a shading tree is pruned or removed—the leaves will sear. Plants can be sunburned, and you will note the brown smears across the leaves when the direct sun hits their fragile surfaces longer than they tolerate.

Large-leafed shade plants can afford the size of their leaves because their environment is shady and moist, and they are assured of continual water to their roots. On the other hand, the stubby, juicy leaf of a succulent, accustomed to living in full sun with little water, stores the water in the leaves, which are small to keep evaporation at the minimum. This leaf physiology indicates how important it becomes for the gardener to carefully mimic the plant's natural home. Not providing water for the shade plant accustomed to moisture threatens its survival because its structure does not allow it to adapt to changed conditions easily or for a long period of time.

Plan the location of plants in the garden using the different textures and colors of leaves to create visual interest.

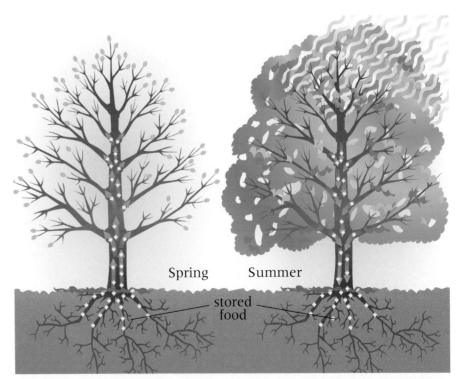

Plants absorb water through their roots—and release it through their leaves. The leaves make the sugars, and send the sugars down to the roots to be stored.

WATERING PRACTICES

A plant is an efficient mechanism, with all its parts designed to provide food and water for its maturation. The roots, like straws, draw water and nutrients out of the soil into the plant. The water is drawn up through the roots and (microscopically) out onto the surface of the leaves. There the sun, or the heat of the day, causes the water to evaporate through the pores. As the water evaporates, it pulls more water through the plant from the roots. This process, called transpiration, explains why a healthy plant that is denied water begins to wilt, and eventually dies from lack of water and nutrition.

Even though plants in the shade may not have bright sunlight shining on their leaves, high evaporation levels occur on hot or windy days. When the leaves lose more water than the roots can quickly replenish, the plant wilts. Except for drought-resistant plants, a properly watered plant is one that has constant access to readily available water. In any garden, shaded or not, it's necessary to increase your watering when the weather turns hot or windy.

Good Watering Practices for Healthy Plants

Plants in the shade may be less resistant to mildews and fungal infections than those in full sun because water stays on their leaves longer. You can

Sprinklers wet the foliage of plants, so it is best to water with this type of irrigation in the morning hours.

limit diseases, however, by being watchful of the time of day you water, and what plants you water when. For example,

To help prevent mildew, water early in the morning so the leaves will be dry by night.

Special attachments for the end of the water hose break the force of the water, allowing it to seep slowly into the ground.

Consistent watering practices are essential for the shade garden.

water begonias or roses (with their mildew-susceptible leaves) early in the day so the leaves dry off by evening. If the weather is hot and dry and your plants are not bothered by mildew, watering at night allows the water to sink into the ground before the daytime temperatures dry it out.

Just as plants can die from too little water, they can die from too much. In order to breathe, roots need oxygen, which they find in the spaces between soil particles. After you water, gravity pulls the water down through the soil and oxy-

gen fills up the spaces again. But when the soil stays soggy because of poor soil texture, oxygen is squeezed out but cannot return because the water doesn't drain. Only water- and bog-loving plants have adapted to having their roots wet continually. Therefore, it is critical that soil in shady areas drain well to maintain healthy roots as it normally dries out slower than soil exposed to sunlight. Working in large quantities of organic soil amendments improves the composition of the soil, creating more spaces between the soil particles so that water drains readily.

In containers, when potting mix fills with water, gravity pulls the water down through the spaces between the particles, allowing oxygen to fill them again. The lack of a drainage hole in a container (or a saucer filled with water) ultimately causes root suffocation and rot. Elevate pots on a

TIP **The Circumference of a Plant's Root Mass**

Although the rule of thumb used to be that the roots of a plant grew out as far as a tree or shrub's dripline (where water would drip down to the ground from the tips of the branches) studies now show that roots may actually extend even farther than that. Irrigate farther than just between the trunk and the dripline to be sure you're doing a thorough job.

layer of pebbles or gravel in the bottom of the saucer so it never sits down in the water.

Oscillating sprinklers allow the ground to absorb more water before it starts to run off.

Sprinklers lose a lot of water to evaporation when it is windy or especially hot and dry.

SOIL PREPARATION

Compost bins come in many shapes and sizes. Any kind works. The keys: Allowing air in and water to drain.

Properly preparing your soil is vital for healthy plants, no matter what kind of garden.

A plant weakened by lack of food or water is more susceptible to diseases and bug infestation. Because the roots draw in water and food from the soil, soil composition plays an important part in delivering nourishment. A good friable soil allows the plant's roots to grow, reaching out for the food and water that nourishes it.

Soil is a mixture of three particles—sand, silt and clay—plus any organic matter that may be present. The silt, clay and organic matter interact with water in the soil and provide the nutrients to the plant root. Sand, although chemically inert, also plays an important role in plant health. The largest in size of the particles, sand creates correspondingly large spaces between the soil particles, which contributes to fast drainage, high oxygen concentrations and good vertical water movement.

Preparing the Soil— Three Points of View

The organic matter in soils is mostly old plant material decomposing under constant attack by bacteria and fungi, which over time liberate mineral elements that are

Autumn is a great time to work on soil preparation—it saves vital time come spring.

essential to plants for their growth. The bacteria and fungi also benefit plants by fighting off microorganisms that cause plant diseases.

Prepare soil thoroughly before setting in new plants. Whether it is just one plant or a whole bed, preparing the planting location properly gets the plant off to a good start.

There are two schools of thought on soil preparation, and like many things in life, they are on opposite sides.

One school uses scientific studies that have discovered that microorganisms in soil, which are helpful to plant health, live in strata particular to the specific microorganism. Turning the soil disrupts their strata, mixing soil from different levels, and consequently the microorganisms die. This team suggests minimal digging ... disrupting the soil minimally. They recommend maintaining a permanent mulch of 6 inches or more that decomposes making the soil as rich and friable as a worked soil.

The other camp proposes loosening the soil to a depth of 24 inches, working it by double-digging, or turning the soil upside down. Quantities of compost and nutrients are worked into the soil, and the whole bed is raised up above the level of the soil. These proponents argue that the original digging benefits the bed for years, and the organic matter reintroduces microorganisms within weeks.

There is a middle road to these two points of view. When digging a bed for planting, a gardener can work the soil just one shovel down, incorporating a great deal of organic matter, compost and soil amendments into the bed. The levels of microorganisms just one shovel down are closer in relationship to each other than to those that live a full 24 inches from the surface.

Plant spring-flowering bulbs such as tulips and narcissus in the autumn.

There are many kinds of fertilizers to choose from.

Adding time-release, pelleted fertilizer once a year and covering the soil with a thick 4- to 6- inch blanket of mulch keeps the soil friable, moist and cool as well as filled with nutrients necessary for healthy plant growth.

Fertilizers

Commercial fertilizers list their contents as the percentage of each nutrient in this order: Nitrogen, phosphorus and potassium (NPK). For example, a formula of 10-10-10 has equal amounts of nitrogen, phosphorus and potassium, while one of 20-20-20 is twice as strong. All-purpose fertilizers have a

Gardeners have a choice of fertilizers— be sure to read the label to find the best for you.

Although the simplest composting method is to let a pile decompose over a year without disturbing it, the three-stage compost pile produces quicker results. Decomposing material is turned when it is moved from bin to bin. Turning aerates the material, causing quicker decay.

How to Plant in the Ground

Transplanting into a huge hole according to the old instructions of digging two times as deep and two times as wide as the rootball may not stimulate good growth, particularly if the hole is filled with soil amendments and fertilizer. Plant roots are lazy, and if they grow round and round in the rich soil, they may not attempt to spread out into the native soil. The result: They become rootbound in the large planting hole.

To plant correctly, dig a hole just a shade wider and deeper than the plant's rootball. Loosen the soil with a spading fork or shovel in the bottom of the hole. Center the plant in the hole and backfill— shovel back in—half the soil you removed. Water the planting hole and gently tamp the soil to make sure there are no air holes. Fill in the rest of the hole, tamp and water again. Mulch with 5 to 6 inches of compost or mulching material. Water daily for at least a week until the feeder roots develop and can support the plant.

balanced formula for the maximum growth of roots, leaves and blooms. For continued healthy plant growth, the gardener must replace nutrients used up by growing plants. Add fertilizer to soil as liquid, powder or pellets that gradually break down so the roots can absorb them. Although it may seem that if some fertilizer is good, more must be better, do not overfertilize plants. As with overfeeding people, too much fertilizer can encourage unhealthy, excess growth.

Recycle trimmings from the garden into the compost. Use compost both for mixing into the soil and for laying down a 3- to 4-inch mulch that helps retain moisture and inhibit weeds.

Matching Fertilizers to Plants

You'll see fertilizers formulated specially for acid-loving plants, which includes many shade plants such as azaleas, ferns and rhododendrons. Fertilizer comes in a variety of forms, from pencil-thick spikes that poke into the soil to granulated formulas that release slowly over several months. Although convenient, spikes are less efficient because their flow of nutrients is limited to the area of their placement. Broadcasting a granulated slow-release pelleted fertilizer around your planting area according to the directions on the container ensures better distribution.

Manufacturers' claims and scientific studies differ on just how long slow-release fertilizers continue to dissolve and release

nutrients in the soil. Watering habits, air and soil temperature and a plant's needs all produce

different effects on the fertilizer's longevity. For the best results add slow-release fertilizer yearly. In mild winter climates, sprinkle out the fertilizer in the late fall. In cold climates, apply just as the weather begins to warm up in early spring.

If you garden in pots and tubs, look for liquid fertilizers that are specially formulated for containers. They include a variety of minerals and supplements important for potted plants. The old organic standby, fish emulsion (which was distinctly fish-fragrant) has now been deodorized, so you can use it for plants indoors and out.

Consider using organic fertilizers in your garden, or pots planted with edible plants. Although there have been no conclusive studies, there are a number of testimonials to the improved taste of vegetables grown using organic fertilizers.

Collect leafmold and other forms of organic matter for your shade garden.

GROWING POTTED GARDENS IN THE SHADE

A shady veranda displays a collection of potted shade plants.

You can grow any plant in a pot. Knowing the specific growth rate of your plant helps you judge the size of the container it needs to keep the roots growing vigorously. A too-small container with less space for root development than a plant needs may stunt the growth of a fast-growing plant so that it never fully develops. Some plants are so willfully vigorous that such stunting doesn't prevent them from flowering or fruiting, although production will be limited compared with a plant grown in the ground. Plants too large or invasive for a small garden can be controlled in pots, but you must root prune regularly (every year or

Shade gardens definitely are not restricted to growing plants in the ground.

This stunning Japanese bonsai must be carefully tended to keep the potting mix from drying out. Yearly root pruning is essential to keep the rootball healthy.

so) to keep the plant from becoming rootbound.

Watering Practices for Containers

Shade container gardening's greatest challenge is keeping pots sufficiently watered throughout the year. Because water so critically affects a plant's life, particularly in a container, water your plants consistently. A drip system on an automatic timer is perhaps the easiest and most reliable way to keep container plants well watered.

Depending upon how extensive a pot collection you have, a simple and inexpensive drip system can be put together with parts bought from a hardware store. A manual system assembles quite easily, and you can hook it up to a garden hose which you turn on daily or several times a week depending upon the weather. There are more elaborate systems run by an electrical timer that water automatically; these are not difficult to install if electricity is handy.

A thin spaghetti tube runs off the main water line to each pot. You can somewhat disguise drip tubing by bringing it up the back of the container; but if you add a tube up through the drainage hole when the pot is planted, it is almost invisible. Raise the plant on bricks or blocks so the tubing is not crimped.

If you do not put your plants on a drip system, water them regularly, digging into the mix with your finger at least 2 inches to make sure that the potting mix is thoroughly moist after watering, not just on the surface. You

may need to drench the pot several times, letting the water fill it up to the rim for better absorption. If the weather becomes windy or hot—which increases the amount of water the plant uses—increase your watering and use a fine mister at least once a day on the plants' leaves.

Polymers/Hydrogels

Particularly useful in maintaining water to moisture-loving, container-grown shade plants is incorporating polymers, sometimes called hydrogels, into the soil mix. In the presence of water, the dry polymer beads swell up into small gelatin-like blobs. As the soil mix dries, the roots can penetrate the polymers to draw out the water as if these were hundreds of small reservoirs of water within the dry soil. After about 10 years, the polymers biodegrade, but until then, they continue to respond

Compost is the best thing to add to any soil, no matter how bad or good the soil may be.

to water, swelling up again and again when moisture comes in contact.

Potting Mixes

Choosing the right mix for the type of plants you raise is essential to produce healthy root growth and, subsequently, healthy plants. Garden soil alone, scooped into pots without careful attention to amendments, will probably not drain well enough to keep your plants alive. Not all commercial potting mixes are the same, for some are designed to drain quickly, and others to retain water longer. A heavy mix with a high proportion of peat moss, by contrast, holds water in the mix and is preferable for shade plants that prefer constantly moist soil.

In garden shops and nurseries, you will find both soil-based mixes and soil-less mixes. Soil-based mixes consist of sterilized soil along with amendments for texture. This soil has been sterilized to rid it of insect eggs, seeds and soil-based fungi.

Although you can sterilize soil in your own oven, the odor of

baking soil may be too strong. If you wish to try it, place 3 to 4 inches of soil in an oven-proof container. Moisten the soil thoroughly, and bake in a 200°F oven until an oven thermometer measures the temperature 180°F in the center of the soil. Some commercial soil-based mixes also have fertilizer added to the mix. Adding more fertilizer to this kind of mix may harm your plants, resulting in burned roots and plant death. The tiny roots of seedlings are particularly sensitive and may not survive fertilizer overdose.

The soil-less mixes are made of peat mixed with sand, perlite or vermiculite. Perlite and vermiculite are minerals heated until they puff up as small particles that provide the proper texture and composition to a mix. Soil-less mixes find favor with gardeners because plants consistently perform well in this kind of mix. The mix provides no nutrition to the plants, so adding fertilizers to aid in plant growth is essential.

Although a majority of plants will grow in an almost neutral mix, many shade plants require an acid mix. The pH balance of a potting mix affects how well a plant absorbs nutrients. Acid plant mixes have a pH of 6.9 and lower; alkaline ones have a pH of 7.1 and higher. Match the pH requirements of your plant with the right mix for best results.

Growing Bulbs in Containers

Bulbs contain all the nutrients they require for the

current year's bloom. After bloom, however, they begin to store up food for the following year. So fertilize flowering bulbs regularly after they have bloomed to ensure flowering performance for the next year.

Never cut off a bulb's green leaves, for the leaves are essential to allow the bulb to process and store nutrients. When the leaves turn yellow, it is safe to cut them away. At that point, you can lift the bulbs out of the container and store them in a cool dry place until you repot them; if they do not crowd the container or are a type that likes to be crowded, you can simply leave them in the container. Store the container in a cool, dry place but check periodically to make sure that snails or slugs didn't travel inside with the container. You may find a bulb that is half-eaten or a snail trail, which looks like a translucent silvery ribbon. Snails and slugs can destroy bulbs by chewing into them whenever they get hungry.

There is no need to water most bulbs while they are dormant. Lily bulbs are an exception, and they should stay in a container which is kept slightly moist throughout the year.

VITAMIN B1

Although touted for years as the means to lessen transplantation shock in plants, studies of Vitamin B1 have shown that it is ineffective in encouraging feeder roots—the fine hair-like roots that absorb nutrients for the plant—to regrow. Although gardeners feel comforted by its use, it does not speed plant recovery. Keeping a transplanted plant well watered while the feeder roots regrow is the most effective means of speeding a plant's recovery.

Mulching Containers

Mulching your containers helps retain moisture in the potting mix and keep the roots cool. A top layer of compost or inert material such as rocks minimize the wind and temperature's drying effect. Compost mulches work best for those plants needing to be kept constantly moist. Keep the mulch back an inch from the stem to prevent keeping the stem too damp. Mulches also help to adjust the pH balance of potting mixes. If you are growing an acid-loving plant, such as a camellia or rhododendron in a container, a mulch of bark or pine needles will decompose to add acidity to the mix.

Containers

A pot's shape affects the amount of room the roots have to grow. Square pots hold a larger volume of potting mix than cylindrical pots with sloping sides. The larger the volume of potting mix, the more room for roots to develop—resulting in a stronger, healthier plant. Some plants, such as daffodils, have long roots, so pots that are deeper than they are wide fit their growing needs

A large plant needs a large pot. The larger the plant, the more extensive its root system. Regularly check the drain hole of your containers to see if roots are beginning to show, indicating that the roots have begun to fill the container. For maximum continued growth of plants—especially vegetable plants, which need continued, rapid development in order to produce their harvest—repot when roots show at the bottom. For ornamentals like vigorously

MULCH

Covering the top of the soil with 2 to 3 inches of organic mulch helps retain moisture, keeps down soil temperature and improves the soil texture. All this allows the roots to wander freely. Plus, a thick 5-inch mulch layer keeps weed seeds from germinating. Any of the following materials makes an effective mulch:

- Bark
- Compost
- Aged, rotted hay
- Alfalfa
- Partially composted leaves
- Pine needles
  (for acid-loving plants}
- Rice hulls
- Aged, rotted straw
- Stones

Tuberous begonias.

growing vines, not repotting can produce the desirable effect of minimizing growth. Plan on root pruning once a year when the plant is dormant in order to avoid a large plant in a smallish pot becoming rootbound, which will inhibit its intake of water and nutrients.

Starting from Seeds

Starting your own plants from seeds is easy, and it offers you the advantage of growing a wide range of varieties that nurseries do not regularly stock as baby seedlings or starter plants. If you live in a cold climate with a short growing season, starting seeds inside produces vigorous plants that are ready for transplanting into outside pots when the weather warms up. You can also sow seeds later in their permanent pots, when the warmth of spring encourages germination and there is no danger of frost.

Check your nursery for seed-starting kits, such as Styrofoam

Concrete and stone pots are very heavy, and are less likely to blow over in a wind.

flats, plastic six-packs or peat pots. Choose pots or containers with individual sections for each seedling so that the transplants will pop out of them easily.

Seeds need temperatures from 65 to 75°F to germinate. Some gardeners place heating mats underneath germinating trays to keep the soil evenly warm. A sunny south window may provide enough warmth and light. If not, hang fluorescent Gro-lights or full-spectrum lights 4 to 6 inches above the containers.

Start your seeds six to eight weeks before you want to put plants outside. Use only packaged, sterilized soil mixes to avoid diseases that infect seedlings. To make sure the plants get off to a good start, add half the recommended amount of an all-purpose slow-release fertilizer to the mix or, once the seedlings are 1 inch high, water them once a week with a low-nitrogen fertilizer diluted to half strength.

Thoroughly moisten the mix with water, then fill the seed container to within 1 inch of the rim. Check the recommended directions on the seed packet and sow the seeds at the correct depth and spacing. After you

TERRA-COTTA

Made of inexpensive low-fired clay, terra-cotta pots have been loved by gardeners for thousands of years. Besides the simple least-expensive unglazed terra-cotta, glazed terra-cotta in shining colors adds beauty to the garden and can be chosen to coordinate with flower bloom. Unglazed pots must be watered more often because the clay breathes and the pores allow moisture to escape, letting the potting mix dry out quicker. This is perfect for plants that like to dry out in between waterings, but less suitable for moisture-loving plants. Unglazed terra-cotta pots are also more susceptible to cold weather, often cracking and crumbling when they freeze.

have sown the seeds, sprinkle or sift mix over the top, to the depth specified on the seed packet. Pat down the mix firmly and water carefully so you don't dislodge the seeds. Keep the mix moist but not soggy to avoid encouraging fungal infections.

Place the seed containers where they get four hours of bright sun a day. If the seedlings begin to stretch up, lean over and look leggy, they are not receiving enough light. When the roots begin to show at the bottom of the container, the young plants are ready to be set out of doors or into larger containers.

Transplanting Young Plants

Because both seedlings and young plants raised indoors or in a greenhouse are tender, you need to accustom them to the more variable temperatures outdoors before you set them out. This process is called "hardening off." For one week before you plant them, set the seedlings outdoors during the day only. Keep them in the shade at first. Then gradually move them into the spot where they will be

planted. When you plant them, do it in the late afternoon to lessen the stress caused by the heat of the day.

How to Plant

To transplant, soak the plants in their pots or flats in a bucket or sink until they stop bubbling. Then gently tap each plant from its container, keeping the rootball and its potting mix intact. Check the required spacing for the plants. Leave enough room around them so they do not become crowded as they mature.

A smaller planting hole more effectively encourages plants to send roots into the surrounding area than a large hole filled with soil amendments and fertilizer. The large hole is like a comfortable bed, and the roots tend to circle around the hole, limiting their access to food and water.

So dig a hole just big enough for the rootball. Loosen the soil at the bottom and at the sides. Set the plant into the hole with the top of the rootball level with the soil and centered in the hole. Backfill the hole with the original soil. Although it's hard

Most nurseries sell plants that are growing in containers. Make sure they have not been in there too long.

to resist, don't fill with soil amendments or fertilizer.

Tamp down the soil firmly around the rootball, making sure the plant is set in securely. Water thoroughly every day for a week to lessen transplanting shock and give the plant time to develop new feeder roots.

How to Pot Up Plants

Almost every container gardening book instructs the reader to add crockery to the bottom of a pot to improve drainage. This instruction uses up all those broken terra-cotta bits most gardeners have lying around, but drainage is actually **imperiled** by this process. The layering of two different materials—the fine-grained potting mix on top and the crockery pieces on the bottom—impedes drainage. The mix drains perfectly well by itself. You can leave the hole at the bottom of the container uncovered if you wish, for after waterings the mix will settle and not fall out. Or you can cover the hole with a flat piece

Grow young plants in a sheltered spot and then transplant to a permanent home.

of crockery or square of nylon screening which retains the mix and prevents snails or slugs from hiding inside the hole.

To pot, first soak the plant in its container in a bucket so that when you tap out the rootball it stays intact and the plant is thoroughly watered, lessening the impact of its switch to a new container. If the plant is too large to fit into a bucket, water it thoroughly by hose. Gauge the amount of potting mix you need to fill the new container and add slow-release fertilizer granules according to the manufacturer's directions. Moisten the mix thoroughly. Add enough mix to the bottom of the new container to allow you to position the top of the rootball an inch below the rim of the container. If you choose to, add hydrogels at this time according to the manufacturer's directions.

Turn the plant on its side or, if size allows, upside down. Tug the plant gently to slide it out of the original container. If it sticks, tap the sides or bottom of the plant sharply. Rootbound plants may be harder to pull out; slide a knife around the sides to help free the plant.

A north-facing house wall hosts a windowbox of pansies.

Center the rootball in the pot and add moistened mix up around the sides. Tamp down the mix and water thoroughly. You may need to add more mix after you have watered to bring the level up to an inch below the rim of the container. Set the plant in a shaded, wind-protected area for several days while the feeder roots grow. Water daily. After three or four days, return the plant to its normal site. Continue to water daily for one week after potting.

Repotting

To keep potted plants healthy, repot them yearly. At this time you can divide overgrown plants, trim the rootball to keep plants from becoming pot-bound or simply move the plant into a larger pot to provide enough room for the next year's growth. Adding fresh potting mix combined with slow-release fertilizer gives the plant a fresh start for the following year. When repotting, examine the roots. Few roots or roots that seem dried or rotten can indicate that you are damaging the

roots either by using too much or too little water.

Plants that have overgrown their containers can be divided and the sections repotted separately. Do this after blooming, but always check the plants' specific requirements because some (like grape hyacinths) prefer to be tightly planted in

HOW TO ROOT PRUNE

Plants that have stayed too long in a container develop tangled roots, twisted around and around the edge of the container. If you replant without root pruning, the plant may stultify and never grow. First try to untangle the roots, straightening them in the process. Assess the roots, and prune off any broken or matted ones. Trim the roots so they are even. Replant as you would a bareroot plant, building a pyramid of soil or potting mix and distributing the roots around the pyramid.

Covering plants when frost threatens helps extend the season in both spring and autumn.

in the fall, after the yearly growth has finished. Repot deciduous plants in the winter, when dormant.

The overgrown roots of a pot-bound plant must be trimmed back and spread out when repotting. Try to untangle the mass of roots, then cut the roots back so that when you repot, you can set them straight into the container without bunching or twisting them. The feeder roots that grow from the tips of the main roots will regrow quite quickly. Put fast-growing plants like vegetables or vines into a much larger container, while slow-growing plants like rhodo-dendron need only the next size up. Add mix to the bottom and the sides of the container, posi-tioning the top of the rootball an inch below the rim of the container. Pat the mix down firmly to eliminate air pockets. Water thoroughly.

their pots; others do not want to be disturbed unless they are dormant. The best time to repot evergreen perennials is

Heavy plants in large con-tainers can be renewed yearly by top dressing. Dig out all the old pot-ting mix you can in the container and measure the amount. Add an appropriate amount of slow-release fertilizer granules to the new potting mix and deposit in the container. Water the container well for the next three to five days, then return to a normal watering schedule.

Frost Protection

Hardy and ten-der are the words that roughly dis-tinguish how well a plant withstands cold. Tender plants

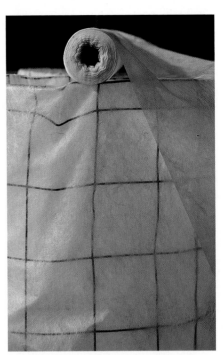

Inexpensive fiber row covers act as miniature greenhouses when draped around row covers or hoops. Although they won't save a plant from freezing if the temperature drops dramatically, they keep the surrounding air temperature 3 to 5 degrees warmer for the plant.

do not tolerate cold tempera-tures because water freezing in the plant tissue expands, dam-aging or destroying the plant. Hardy plants can stand up to a certain amount of cold and are often described as hardy to a certain temperature—for example, "hardy to 32°F." A third category, half-hardy plants, will usually survive a cold spell but may not survive extended cold weather. Protect plants in the ground with heavy mulches of straw or compost.

Plants in containers are more susceptible to the cold and wind chill factors. Move containers to sheltered areas. Container-grown deciduous plants can overwinter in a basement because while in dormancy they do not need light or water. Toward the end of winter water and bring out to the light as the weather warms up.

Windbreaks are important to help in protecting plants from the wind's drying effects.

PESTS AND DISEASES

Caterpillars can quickly mow a plant down to nothing. These pests can turn into beneficial butterflies, though.

A variety of different pests may attack your plants. Try to identify the problem before you use any sprays or poisons, because insecticides only work for specific types of pests. Take the affected plant or leaves to your local nursery or cooperative extension agent for identification. A number of insects, such as aphids or mites, can be washed off with a brisk spray of water; repeat as necessary. A mild infestation of scale can be scraped off with your fingernail or the back of a knife.

Using Non-Toxic Pesticides

For edible plants, try the new series of organic soap-based pes-ticides that suffocate pests with fatty acids that are harmless to people and animals. Commercially available biological controls, such as lacewings and trichogramma wasps (very tiny and not like their larger annoying relatives) attack plant pests without bothering humans. But those voracious eaters of plant pests, the familiar ladybird beetles, are less successful when purchased and introduced into a garden. The majority generally fly away in a day or two. Consider using *Bacillus thuringiensis* (Bt), a bacteria

spray that kills caterpillars with-out leaving any harmful residue. Although protecting your

Grasshoppers are one of the hardest insects to deal with in the garden because they are so mobile.

harvest by organic methods may be slightly more labor-intensive, it is better for the environment. And growing safe and nutritious food for yourself and your family is a clear incentive in the case of edibles.

Slugs and snails can become persistent in the spring and fall and under moist conditions. Maintain a vigilant watch, going out in the evening with a flashlight to hand-pick slugs and snails; drop them into a bag containing several generous scoops of salt. When finished discard the bag, tightly tied, into the garbage. Snail traps, such as a tipped-over clay pot container with room for them to crawl into after their night strolls, will garner a collection for you. There are effective snail baits low in toxicity; but for safety's sake, do not scatter them on the ground. Place the bait in an empty juice container lying on its side on the ground. The snails and slugs will collect there at night. Discard the container when it is full.

Earwigs, those ¹/₂-inch-long, dark brown insects with the

Many diseases affect plants. Spotting on leaves is often caused by fungi and bacteria. Consult reference books or a county extension agency to deal with diseases.

pincers at the end of their body, love to perforate tender leaves with dainty and not-so-dainty holes. Roll up a newspaper loosely and leave it out in the garden at night. In the morning, shake out the earwigs and step on them. It may take several nights for your earwig colony to

move into the newspaper hotel, but persevere.

Plant Diseases

Viruses and fungi also attack plants, creating stunted and sometimes unusually colored plants. The shade garden's moist atmosphere can encourage mildew and fungus attacks. Good air circulation helps plants combat fungal diseases. Pinch-pruning any stems that cross into the center of a plant can help circulation. Larger plants may need more severe pruning to open them up. At the end of the summer, some annuals such as impatiens and begonias are particularly susceptible to fungus because they are at the end of their life cycle. Replace the annuals with fall-blooming plants and let the bulbs dry out in preparation for winter storage.

Hand-picking large insects is an environmentally friendly form of pest control.

FURTHER READING

Brickell, Christopher, Editor-in-Chief.
The American Horticultural Society Encyclopedia of Garden Plants.
New York. Macmillan Publishing Company, 1989.

Druse, Ken.
The Natural Shade Garden.
New York. Clarkson Potter, 1992.

Hobhouse, Penelope.
Penelope Hobhouse's Gardening through the Ages.
New York. Simon & Schuster, 1992.

Kourik, Robert.
Designing and Maintaining Your Edible Landscape Naturally.
Santa Rosa, California. Metamorphic Press, 1986.

Sackville-West, Vita V.
Sackville-West's Garden.
New York. Atheneum, 1986.

Sunset National Garden Book.
Menlo Park, California. Sunset Books, Inc., 1997.

SOURCES

Anderson Design
P.O. Box 4057-C
Bellingham, WA 98227
(800)947-7697
Website: andesign@pacificrim.net
A variety of arches, arbors and trellises in kits or plans

K. Van Bourgondien Bulbs and Perennials
P.O. Box 1000
Babylon, NY 11702-9004
(800)552-9996, FAX (515)660-1228
Internet orders: www.dutchbulbs.com
An extensive collection of hostas and bulbs

Country Casual Garden
17317 Germantown Rd.
Germantown, MD 20874-2999
(800)284-8325, FAX (301)540-7354
E-mail: sales@countrycasual.com
A good mail-order source for garden furnishings

Cook's Garden
P.O. Box 535
Londonderry, VT 05148
(800)457-9703
Excellent vegetable seeds especially lettuces and mesclun mixes

Fancy Fronds
P.O. Box 1090
Gold Bar, WA 98251
(350)793-1472
Hardy ferns from all over the world

Jackson & Perkins Seeds of Change
P.O. Box 15700
Santa Fe, NM 87506
(888)762-7333
Internet orders: jacksonandperkins.com
Mail-order source for iceberg roses

Johnny's Selected Seeds
Foss Hill Rd.
Albion, ME 04810
(207)437-9297, FAX (800)437-4290
Website: www.johnnyseeds.com
An excellent catalog for a wide variety of vegetable seeds

Lilypons Water Gardens
P.O. Box 10
6800 Lilypons Rd.
Buckeystown, MD 21717-0010
(800)999-5459, FAX (800)879-5459
Website: www.lilypons.com
An excellent range of plants and supplies for the water or bog garden

Shady Oaks Nursery, Plants for Shady Places
112 10 Ave. S. E.
Waseca, MN 56093-3122
(800)594-8006, FAX (888)735-4531
Internet orders:
    http://www.shadyoaks.com
Most desirable shade plants

Smith and Hawken
117 East Strawberry Drive
Mill Valley, CA 94941
(800)776-3336
Website: www.smith-hawken.com
Tools, irrigation supplies, garden furniture, trellises and pergolas

Stokes Tropicals
P.O. Box 9868
New Iberia, LA 70562-9868
(800)624-9706, FAX (318)365-6991
Website: www.stokestropicals.com
The catalog focuses on tropical plants

Territorial Seed Catalog
P.O. Box 157
Cottage Grove, OR 97424-0061
(541)942-9547, FAX (888)657-3131
Web Site: www.territorial-seed.com
Excellent short-season vegetable seeds

Vintage Wood Works
P.O. Box R
High 34 South
Quinlan, TX 78624
(903)356-2158, FAX (903)356-3023
Kits for Victorian gazebos and other garden buildings

Vixen Hill Gazebos
Main Street
Elverson, PA 19520
(800)235-3136, FAX (215)286-2099
Kits for gazebos in Victorian or colonial styles

PLANT HARDINESS ZONE MAP

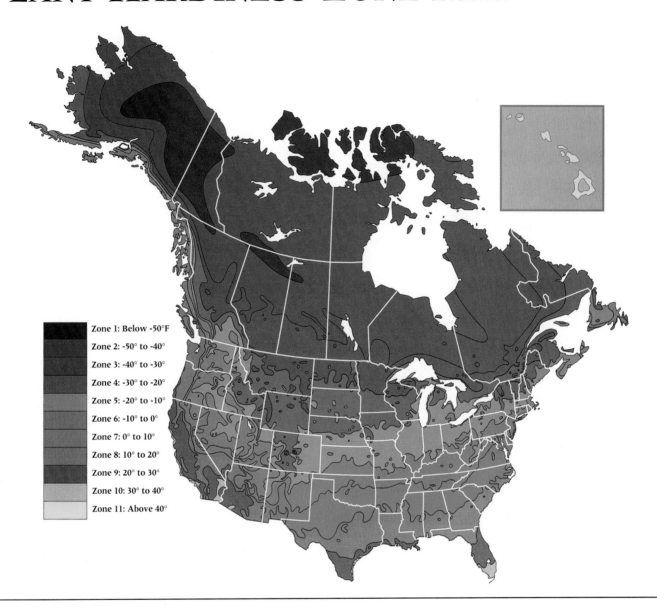

Zone 1: Below -50°F
Zone 2: -50° to -40°
Zone 3: -40° to -30°
Zone 4: -30° to -20°
Zone 5: -20° to -10°
Zone 6: -10° to 0°
Zone 7: 0° to 10°
Zone 8: 10° to 20°
Zone 9: 20° to 30°
Zone 10: 30° to 40°
Zone 11: Above 40°

INDEX OF PLANTS

GENERAL INDEX